P9-BBV-548

THE SNARE

LOIS MOWDAY
THE SNARE

NAVPRESS
A MINISTRY OF THE NAVIGATORS
P.O. BOX 6000, COLORADO SPRINGS, COLORADO 80934

The Navigators is an international Christian organization. Jesus Christ gave His followers the Great Commission to go and make disciples (Matthew 28:19). The aim of The Navigators is to help fulfill that commission by multiplying laborers for Christ in every nation.

NavPress is the publishing ministry of The Navigators. NavPress publications are tools to help Christians grow. Although publications alone cannot make disciples or change lives, they can help believers learn biblical discipleship, and apply what they learn to their lives and ministries.

Library of Congress Catalog Card Number:
87-63506
ISBN 08910-91556

Second printing, 1988

Printed in the United States of America

To Lisa and Lara

This is my prayer: that your love may abound more and more in knowledge and depth of insight, so that you may be able to discern what is best *and may be pure and blameless until the day of Christ, filled with the fruit of righteousness that comes through Jesus Christ—to the glory and praise of God.*

Philippians 1:9-11

Contents

Acknowledgments

There are so many to thank for their love, prayers, and encouragement. Naming names is so risky—I know I will forget one dear to me. But you know who you are:

The two who, in love, hold me to a high level of accountability; the prayer warrior with the direct line to God; the godly, young woman who is an exemplary role model for my daughters; the willing friends who allowed me to quote them; the publishing team that makes me feel very special; the ones who call just to encourage me to persevere as a writer; my parents, who taught me moral principles by living them in front of me; my children, who *always* encourage me in *everything*; a "you told me so" thank you to my first mentor who saw more in a scrawled note than a scrawled note; and my most recent mentor, who brings Paris cafés to Colorado.

Author

Lois Mowday was married for over thirteen years when her husband, Jack, was killed in a tragic hot-air balloon accident. Testimony of the grace of God in that tragedy led to numerous speaking and writing opportunities.

For five years with Jack, and for three years after his death, Lois was a teacher-trainer in the Evangelism Explosion Ministry of the Coral Ridge Presbyterian Church in Ft. Lauderdale, Florida.

Lois has given her testimony at a Billy Graham Crusade in Indianapolis and at a Luis Palau Crusade in Colorado Springs. She has had articles published in *Decision Magazine, Moody Monthly,* and *Christianity Today.*

Lois is a frequent speaker at Christian women's groups, seminars, and Bible studies. She has two daughters, Lisa and Lara, and lives in Colorado Springs.

Introduction

This book is not written from an ivory tower. It is written by someone like you, who struggles frequently with temptation.

I was married for over thirteen years before my husband was killed in a tragic hot-air balloon accident. For the past seven years, I have been a widow. During this time I've returned to the "dating scene." It hasn't been easy. My own walk with the Lord is not blameless. But His grace, love, and forgiveness have encouraged me to put into writing some principles I have learned to be true.

Though the names used in this book are fictitious, the illustrations are based on actual incidents.

May something in this book enable you to see a little more of Jesus and more closely walk with Him.

PART I

An Essential Question

ONE

Why . . . and Why Ask Why?

The attractive young woman sat across from me in the hotel coffee shop—head down, tears flowing. I had been at a speaking engagement out of town and knew her only casually. She was embarrassed to talk honestly with someone who was practically a stranger, but her pain couldn't be contained.

"I'm sorry. I didn't mean to break down so quickly," she said.

"It's okay," I replied with a slight nod that I hoped communicated my own sorrow at her obvious turmoil.

"My husband left me for another woman. I never want to see him again! But, I don't know what to do with the hurt."

We talked for a while. She admitted that she had seen a few men—only as friends—since her husband had moved out of the house.

And, there had been one affair.

She assured me that it had been nothing serious, and that it was over. She had simply responded to a kind and dear friend who was there in a painful, lonely moment.

Before I could respond, she said, "*Why* is it wrong to want a little comfort—to just be with someone who cares?"

Why, indeed?

Why ask why?

This woman, her husband, the woman with whom he was involved, and that woman's husband were all professing Christians. The scenario is not a new one. The breakdown of family units due to infidelity is all too common, even among Christians. The instance of immorality among singles is also on the upswing.

Only a few years ago, a person professing to be a Christian would rarely have come right out and asked why immorality is wrong. There was an acceptance in the evangelical community that morality was still a lifestyle to be desired. In fact, it was not considered as an option. It was a biblical standard that went along with being a Christian. There were certainly people caught in this particular trap, but the acceptance of morality as a necessary part of the Christian lifestyle was secure.

Now that we find ourselves in the middle of a culture that no longer views immorality as a sin, we need to go back for a moment and see why it is important to even address this issue.

Definition of adultery and fornication

In Exodus 20:14, the text says, "You shall not commit adultery." The word adultery is associated with the turning aside of Israel from the true God to the worship of idols.

According to *Webster's New Collegiate Dictionary,* adultery means "voluntary sexual intercourse between a married man and someone other than his wife or between a married woman and someone other than her husband." Fornication means, "sexual intercourse between unmarried people."

The biblical definition has an added implication of an offense toward God: not only the breaking of His law, but an attitude of turning from Him and to something or someone else. God provided that within the institution of marriage, sexual intercourse was not considered to be worshiping someone other than God. Outside of marriage, however, our own desires become of primary importance and are compared to the description in the Old Testament of the sin of idol worship.

In the context of marriage, sexual intercourse is part of, a reflection of, a fulfillment of a commitment to another person and to God. When sexual intercourse takes place apart from that commitment, an individual's own interests slip into first place in his or her heart. We do not see much in the form of worship before statues today, but we are surrounded by the all-consuming worship of *self.*

Why not accept immorality as a part of a Christian lifestyle?
The definitions of adultery and fornication give us our first and most obvious answer as to why we should not commit immoral acts: because God forbids them.

Somehow, as I looked at the hurting woman across the table from me, I knew that to tell her she could not have a moment of comfort in the arms of a man because God had forbidden it would fall on deaf ears. She already knew that. Her pain was so great, however, that the letter of the law was not enough to keep her from grasping that one disobedient moment.

God does say that we should not be sexually immoral, and that should be enough. It is enough. It is all the reason we need. *But*—we all know that we are incapable of keeping the law. If we have a relationship with Christ, which frees us from the letter of the law, then why be so worried about not keeping this particular commandment? Because Christ asked us to follow Him and His example. He asked us to keep His commandments because we love Him. We are not to keep them to earn something; we cannot do that. But, we are to keep them because of a heart motivated by love.

My friend in the coffee shop knew that God forbids adultery. She knew she shouldn't do it. She even knew what had caused her to feel the way she did. (Causes are discussed in Part II.)

After we talked some more, it became evident that knowing alone was not enough for her to change her behavior. We talked about the inevitable pain that would result from the affair. She was reluctant to admit that there would be any. She reminded me that it was nothing and that it was over. Little phrases of defensiveness crept into her conversation. The beginnings of guilt. The pain of guilt had been overshadowed by the pain of rejection by her husband. But—it would surface sooner or later.

The bottom-line why
The consequences of disobeying God, guilt, and pain are three valid reasons to live a moral life. Because we are selfish, however, we have a capacity to lay these all aside. God will forgive, guilt will be justified, pain will be lessened by the comfort of the immoral relationship.

Almost true. God *will* forgive. But God is a person with whom we have a relationship on *His* terms. His terms are that we are either for

Him or against Him. We accept all of His Word or we jeopardize our relationship with Him. If we have accepted Jesus Christ, we are forgiven. We will sin, but our sins are forgiven.

But—we cannot arbitrarily take a commandment and give up on it. To do so is to say that God is right in nine out of ten cases. Either we accept God to be infinitely wise in all His requests or we deem ourselves wiser than He. God's Word is not a negotiable contract. We do not have the option to go to God and make a counter offer. Because God is who He is, though, we can accept His Word as the very best possible way for us to live.

It is interesting that our society severely punishes in three of the four commandments relating to actions: murder, stealing, and lying. But it does not punish adultery nearly as harshly. (The other commandments have to do with offenses toward God or attitudes of the heart such as honor and covetousness.) We need to take note that the Bible refers to adultery in the same manner that it refers to murder, stealing, and lying:

> "Will you steal and murder, commit adultery and perjury, burn incense to Baal and follow other gods you have not known, and then come and stand before me in this house, which bears my Name. . . ?" (Jeremiah 7:9-10)

> Hear the word of the LORD, you Israelites, because the LORD has a charge to bring against you who live in the land: "There is no faithfulness, no love, no acknowledgment of God in the land. There is only cursing, lying and murder, stealing and adultery . . . ." (Hosea 4:1-2)

> Nor did they repent of their murders, their magic arts, their sexual immorality or their thefts. (Revelation 9:21)

Would my friend across the table be asking me why it would be wrong for her to rob a bank if she were broke and starving? I doubt it. She would certainly be seeking relief, but not by stealing. Would she be asking me why she couldn't kill her husband because of what he had done to her? She might feel like killing him, but I doubt that she would seriously consider it.

Why?

One of the reasons is that in our society, it is still considered wrong and is punishable to steal and murder. In cases of the law (in the courtroom, contracts, etc.), it is wrong and punishable to lie. Punishment is a pretty strong motivation to keep someone from doing something. But even beyond that, our society looks upon such offenders as having somewhat less than desirable character. They are not viewed in ways that most of us want to be viewed.

Immorality has slipped out of the company of its dark companions and has become part of the norm of the day. Social consciousness does return when we have a political candidate caught in an immoral act. When it comes to trusting someone with the future of the country, we prefer that his moral character be in line with traits like honesty, integrity, and honor. Yet for the most part, immorality is not considered a vice, but more of a weakness, or even a prowess, depending on the point of view.

The bottom-line *why* we have to answer depends on our relationship with the Lord. As our time together ended, my friend asked, "What should I do?"

"You need to make a decision. You need to decide if you are going to walk with the Lord or if you are not. If you are, immorality is a lifestyle that you have to give up. It won't be easy or instant. But first you need to say *yes* to trying again to put the Lord first."

She had tasted of the Lord and remembered that He was good.

"I want to, but I don't know how," she whispered.

"Knowing how will come. The first step, today, is to acknowledge the desire to change."

She nodded a silent "yes." As I looked at her, I ached for her, for the battle ahead. At the same time, I felt an excitement in knowing that if she really could begin to untangle the damaged emotions controlling her, she would experience a new power and a deeper relationship with the Lord. The road ahead was uphill and long. The end results would prove to be well worth the effort.

PART II

Causes of Immorality

Counselor after involvement with counselee: "We'd been married six years and had two children when we started seminary in California. My wife concentrated on the kids; I was consumed with study, secular work, and weekend ministry. We grew apart. The pattern continued in our first pastorate. She raised the children; I studied, preached, taught Bible classes, and counseled. Then a crisis threatened an end to my ministry. I was put in a vulnerable situation. At that time, I found it easier to turn to women I had counseled than to my wife."

Christian woman after marriage ended: "My marriage ended suddenly. I knew I was in a vulnerable position, but I didn't really know what that meant. I became emotionally dependent on a good friend. I know now that being vulnerable means that you have to be very careful not to depend on someone in an unhealthy way."

Christian businessman after involvement with coworker: "Unless a person is actually out looking for an affair, I would say the biggest cause of immorality is vulnerability. . . . The biggest obstacle in overcoming the danger of a vulnerable situation is a lack of communication with your spouse."

Pastor after involvement with church member: "I personally have a need to be a hero. I need to be the guy with the answers, who can solve your problems—the guy who can really take care of you. That's my messiah complex. As a result, when I see someone hurting, I want to fill that need. When there is a response to that action, it lays someone like me open to a real vulnerability."

Christian woman after broken relationship with her husband: "I was in such pain that I wanted to get relief. I did not understand how really vulnerable I was to doing something stupid. I was not on guard. I just wanted relief from the pain of loss and loneliness."

(NOTE: The quotes that begin many of the chapters are from people who were involved in part of the process that can lead to immorality. They are direct quotes, though written anonymously. They stand alone, needing no explanation. Personal experience is one of the best teachers. May we all learn from these insights.)

TWO
Vulnerability

Threatened security

Marc woke with a start. He was sweating.

"I must have had a nightmare," he thought.

Then he remembered. The nightmare was true. Today was the day that he had to go into the same office but assume a new job.

His boss had called it a "change," a "lateral move." But everyone, including Marc, knew it was a step down. He was simply not producing to the level desired in his old position.

He got out of bed with less-than-enthusiasm for the day that lay ahead of him. Annie was downstairs making breakfast; the kids already off to school. He hated to face Annie. She had been the kind of wife a man prays for, but he felt so inadequate this morning. The news of his demotion had been as much a shock to her as to Marc, but she had responded well. She had tried to hide her disappointment and encourage him to hang in there.

Now she was smiling at him from across the table. He was grateful for her attitude, but it didn't really help to lift his crushed spirit.

"Well, off to face the music—or should I say humiliation?" he said as he headed out the door.

As Marc drove to work, the sense of dread intensified. He simply could not dismiss the reality that he was in a situation that he would do almost anything to get out of. He felt like a complete failure. No amount of positive self-talk helped.

He made it through that first day with awkward attempts to hide his discomfort. The days that followed didn't get much better. His choices seemed very limited, so he kept going in, kept trying. The only bright spot was his administrative assistant. She was smart and competent. She praised him openly and soon had him believing in himself again. Marc began to rely on her. He began to rely on her for much more than work-related help. She soon became an emotional support that he eagerly responded to.

It wasn't long before his attachment led to an involvement he had not intended. He loved his wife, he loved his family. But this lovely, encouraging woman had really been there for him in his time of great need.

Rejection rebound

Elaine had decided not to date for a while. The breakup with Tim had been too painful and she knew she was in a vulnerable position. She threw herself into her work and purposely filled weekend nights with dinners with girlfriends or movies.

The pain didn't go away. "Time heals all wounds" didn't seem to be working. One of Elaine's friends wanted her to meet a man that the friend worked with. He was single and interested in meeting someone just on a friendship basis. After some persuasion, Elaine agreed to a blind date. The evening was enjoyable, no big thrill, but nice. "Yes," Elaine told herself, "it was nice to get out—and nothing heavy happened. He was nice, but no bells."

Elaine realized (she *thought*) that she was over the emotional hurt of the breakup with Tim. The pain subsided and she was having a good time with a new "friend." They began to spend more and more time together and soon a serious involvement resulted. Elaine was far more involved than she should have been—and she knew it—but she didn't know how she had gotten there or how to get out.

Vulnerability means added risk.

Being vulnerable, according to *Webster's,* means to be "open to attack or damage; assailable." There is a positive definition of vulnerability: openness with people we can trust, along with commitment to the Lord and to each other. That is not what we are referring to here.

The kind of vulnerability we're talking about is the result of a circumstance, relationship, or change that has left us wounded or weary. Because we are emotionally run down, our defenses are down. Often our perspective on things is clouded. We are not able to make judgments based on truth. Everything is seen through an emotional filter. Pain is intensified. Therefore, the pursuit of relief from pain is also intensified.

When you are vulnerable, a situation that might otherwise be safe may now be unsafe. I had a skiing accident this past season. My knee was operated on and is now in the process of healing. I *could* ski now, but it would be very risky. Even an easy run presents a danger to my damaged knee. Before my accident, an easy run was just that—an easy run. With a weakness in my knee, I have to exercise extra caution. I cannot ski as if I had never been hurt. Situations that cause vulnerability result in the same kind of need: a need to evaluate the added risk and to adjust responses accordingly.

Threatened security and the end of a relationship are vulnerable situations used in the previous examples. There are a host of others. Many of them are not real obvious. Something as simple as a minor health problem can wear down our defenses. One dangerous adversary whose harmful effects are beginning to be widely recognized is *stress*. The source of stress in a person's life can be difficult to detect. Because we all handle different situations with different degrees of ease or difficulty, what is stressful to one person may be non-stressful to another. People in the military who become used to moving a great deal may not find that a particularly stressful process. However, another family who has lived in the same place for a number of years may find a move a major source of stress.

One of the most common forms of stress that leads to broken relationships is that of burnout. When a person is exhausted, he is in a very vulnerable position. He simply cannot think as clearly as someone who is healthy. Christian work often contributes greatly to burnout because of the nature of the work. It seems to be more difficult to cut down on one's work load when the work is so closely related to helping others. We need to realize that helping others at the expense of our own health and the well-being of our families is not what God intended. God certainly never meant for anyone to work so hard for the Kingdom that he becomes unable to fight off the enemy.

When Gordon MacDonald, former president of Inter-Varsity

Christian Fellowship, was asked what contributed to his adultery, part of his answer was, "I was desperately weary in spirit and body. . . ."[1]

A biblical example of a man suffering from burnout was Elijah.

> Elijah was afraid and ran for his life. When he came to Beersheba in Judah, he left his servant there, while he himself went a day's journey into the desert. He came to a broom tree, sat down under it and prayed that he might die. "I have had enough, LORD," he said. "Take my life; I am no better than my ancestors." Then he lay down under the tree and fell asleep.
>
> All at once an angel touched him and said, "Get up and eat." He looked around, and there by his head was a cake of bread baked over hot coals, and a jar of water. He ate and drank and then lay down again.
>
> The angel of the LORD came back a second time and touched him and said, "Get up and eat, for the journey is too much for you." (1 Kings 19:3-7)

Elijah was so tired that he wanted to die. He had a major case of burnout. The Lord, instead of taking his life, provided a broom tree for him to rest under. Then He provided food and water—and more rest. Sometimes we simply have to stop everything and crawl under a broom tree. We may have to return to, or rest in the middle of, a bad situation. But after the rest, our ability to handle the stress in a godly way will be increased.

So often, we think we simply cannot take the time to lay responsibilities aside to rest. When "the journey is too much," we must pull back or the job at hand will not be achieved successfully anyway.

Recognize your weakness.

We often have little control over the situations of life that cause us to be vulnerable. They are not things we choose, and they are things we would change if we could. But, here we are: emotionally down, physically weary, afraid, hurt. What can we do to prevent seeking comfort from the wrong source in these situations?

The first thing we have to do is recognize where we are. If we find ourselves saying things like—"I'm hurt"; "I'm weary"; "I'm disappointed"; "I'm afraid"; "I deserve better"; "I can't take it any longer";

"I'm alone"—then we are in danger of falling into a compromising situation.

If we recognize we are in a position to be easily attacked, we can be prepared. We can determine to move very cautiously because we *know* that our judgment is impaired. Elijah couldn't go on with his journey until he rested. Sometimes we cannot make decisions because we are so vulnerable, and thus likely to make wrong ones.

The danger with relationships when we are vulnerable is that we may not be able to evaluate them honestly and from a godly perspective. What is bitter may look sweet because of our weakened position. So often, we see people come out of a broken relationship and hastily enter another relationship. The problem is one of our giving damaged emotions enough time to heal. This affects our judgment, and the new relationship may not be seen clearly. In finding relief in relationships with other people, we may also short-circuit the Lord's working in our life when He is trying to meet our needs Himself.

Hurt takes time to heal. In trying to shorten that time, we may simply put a Band-Aid on a severe wound and say it is healed. Though we say it is healed, when that wound receives another blow, the pain is even greater than before. One bad situation covered over by an ungodly relationship will only result in more pain than the first situation ever produced.

Alternatives

In the first illustration, if Marc had been aware of his vulnerability, he might have prevented his involvement with his administrative assistant. He could have been cautious in the way he responded to her praise. He could also have sought more comfort from his wife, who was willing to be supportive. With time and the help of some godly counsel, he could have come to realize that his self-worth was not based on his job in the first place. In building up his relationship with the Lord, he could have regained his perspective of worth based on that relationship.

After the end of a relationship like that of Elaine and Tim, time is probably the best remedy for the healing of damaged emotions. Although time does not completely heal all wounds, it certainly aids our perception of truth. It is risky to enter another relationship on the heels of a broken one. Waiting (a tough thing to do), focusing on other things, and trusting that the Lord will take care of future hopes is much safer than looking at a new person to take the pain away.

Precautions to take

If you are in a vulnerable situation, recognize that your judgment may be impaired.

Determine to live by biblical standards no matter how tough the situation gets.

Look for rationalization in your thinking. Don't allow yourself to rationalize ungodly behavior for any reason.

Move slowly and cautiously in making any decisions. Seek counsel from trusted friends who are committed Christians walking closely with the Lord.

Decrease your work load, if at all possible.

Enter into a relationship of accountability with a friend who is a mature Christian walking with the Lord.

Maintain the basics: Stay in the Word, have quiet times, pray, and be in the fellowship of believers who are walking with the Lord.

Do not take even a small step in the direction of a relationship that may lead to ungodly behavior.

Pray for protection, pray for discernment, pray for rest, draw close to the Lord in ways that allow you to begin to feel His presence. Abide, read, talk to Him, think about Him, focus on Jesus.

THREE

Denial

All is well.

"We never fight," Diane would beam her big, convincing smile as she made one of her typical declarations about the condition of her marriage. Her audience would inevitably ask how they managed such incredible harmony after so many years, and Diane would state that they just understood each other and seemed to have no trouble agreeing.

If Bob were with her, he would refrain from comment (he was a quiet man) but would in no way disagree with her. He was used to Diane being "center stage" when they were out—and center stage when they were at home. She basically ran the show. Bob had never challenged the arrangement. He agreed that they had a good marriage and seemed content to be in the background. "I *am* a quiet man," he would think to himself, "without many needs, just taking life one day at a time."

On occasion, Diane's friends would ask her about the lack of communication in her marriage, and she would deny that there was any lack. "He is just quiet, and we happen to agree on most things." Diane's friends didn't buy that answer, but they had come to accept it.

Bob's friends knew he was an unhappy man. He never complained, but he seldom expressed any joy either. They had tried to break through the wall of denial with him on a few occasions, but he wouldn't budge. After twenty years of a smooth-sailing marriage and a successful medical career, why upset things?

Diane always accompanied Bob on business trips and conventions. He would not have thought of leaving her behind. After years of a conflict-free schedule, they finally hit a snag. They had registered for an important medical meeting in California. Two weeks before they were to attend this meeting in California, a church seminar that Diane was coordinating had to reschedule and the new date fell on the same days as the medical meeting. Bob had to go to California. Diane *had* to stay home.

They didn't argue. They solved it amicably. Of course. Bob would attend his first meeting without Diane on his arm. Diane was disappointed, but felt the importance of her meeting warranted such action. Bob didn't express feelings one way or the other.

Bob's buddies kidded him about his first "free" trip. He smiled faintly, but had no further response. "What's all the fuss?" he thought. "No one notices me when she is around. Why would this be any different?"

But it *was* different. She appeared to his left at the opening session. She was a pediatrician from the East Coast. Her husband had not joined her—he seldom joined her. She asked Bob about his practice. She asked him his thoughts on the speaker. She smiled. She seemed really interested in what Bob had to say. She listened and listened. She complimented.

Bob responded.

When Bob returned home, he looked back on that week and couldn't understand how his perfect marriage had been invaded. He had denied for years what he wanted and needed until it came from out of nowhere. Now, as he looked at Diane he saw so much of what had been wrong. "Why hadn't he seen it before?" He tried to talk to Diane about his feelings, but she was completely bewildered. He did not tell her of the affair, but he was no longer content in their "perfect" marriage.

Diane and Bob separated. She continued to deny that there was anything *really* wrong. She insisted that all he needed was some space. Denial after denial.

There are no needs.

Jill had grown up in a time when it was especially popular to get good grades and live by high standards. She had done both to the praise of her peers and parents. Her self-image was secure as a young woman who knew where she was going and was doing it with integrity and character.

On Jill's thirtieth birthday, her girlfriends from work threw her a surprise party. "You're getting up there, Jill," they teased. "Where is that ring on your finger?"

"You know me," she responded. "I'm not that interested in snagging a man."

Her lack of dating was an office joke, but not intended disrespectfully. Jill was attractive and competent. Her coworkers assumed she did not date because she did not *want* to date. She told herself she did not date because she had no need for male companionship. If that had been true, it would have been okay. But it wasn't. Jill denied the need to date in order to handle the fact that she wasn't asked out. She never looked at herself and her situation to see why else she might not have been asked out.

In her thirtieth year, Jill also celebrated a job promotion. She was excited as she reported to her new supervisor with enthusiasm. He was a vice-president with the company, someone who demanded near-perfection. Jill felt confident that she could deliver. He was married, all-business—a "safe" man.

The compliments were, at first, centered around her work. She enjoyed the praise, remembering her high school years of stardom. The personal compliments began slowly and innocently—so they both thought.

In a matter of months, the inevitable happened. The needs that Jill had so long denied were being met by a man who had no right to meet them.

This can't be wrong.

Sue and Ted first met in college. They had been good friends—that was all. Now, ten years later, they found themselves working for the same organization. Sue was divorced and Ted had never married, so they began to see each other. Ted had not found a church home so Sue invited him to join her.

They enjoyed each other socially, at work and at church. They felt that they had a balanced relationship that enhanced them individually. Neither of them intended to slip into a sexually immoral relationship, but neither of them was convicted that it was terribly wrong either. After all, they were two consenting adults, they were both free, and they were committed to the Lord in all other areas.

They didn't discuss marriage and they kept their sexual involvement a secret. Everything went along fine for a while. Then Ted started to spend less and less time with Sue. She questioned and complained. He gave weak excuses, but the relationship began to deteriorate. Sue was devastated when she learned that Ted was seeing someone else.

Their relationship had not been right before God, and now it was ending. Sue continued denying to herself that their behavior had been wrong and suffered greatly wondering why Ted had left. But Ted had a series of relationships similar to the one with Sue.

Both of them denied that sin was sin, and therefore never acknowledged the results of living outside the will of God.

Denial comes in two varieties.

Denying that there are any problems or needs can lead to an uncontrolled satisfying of those needs at an unexpected moment, in an unexpected way.

Imagine that a child is outside playing and lunch time is approaching. The child is hungry but he doesn't want to miss the fun and interrupt his play. So, he says he isn't hungry. Let's further suppose that his mother allows him to miss lunch. By late afternoon, he is really hungry, but continues to play and tell himself that he is not hungry.

Around 5 p.m. an ice cream truck comes along. The child hears the bells of the truck and can deny his hunger no longer. He buys a large chocolate cone and hurriedly gobbles it down. He feels immediate satisfaction—in fact, he doesn't want his dinner now because he feels full. Suppose again that his mother is not the "mother-of-the-year" and allows him to skip dinner. By around 8 p.m. he doesn't feel so good. His stomach aches and he feels queasy.

His denied hunger surfaced at the sound of the ice cream truck bell. He met that need with a poor substitute for what he really needed. Then, because he was full of the wrong solution, he didn't want what was truly good for him. So, he passed up something good and felt worse than ever later.

Refusing to acknowledge that a sin is a sin is also a dangerous form of denial.

There is an illustration that compares accepting Christ to taking a bath. You do not get clean and then take a bath. You take a bath to get clean. When you accept Christ you do not clean up your act *first.* You accept Christ and then He enables you to begin to clean it up. Taking the illustration a step further, suppose you are getting ready to take a bath and you remember a bad cut on your arm. You know that the soap and water will make the cut hurt again, so you cover it securely with a large Band-Aid. You take the bath and all is well—you are clean and the cut is protected. This routine continues for a number of days. The cut doesn't seem to be healing. In fact, it is getting noticeably worse. The dirt in it that was never cleaned out has caused an infection. You are told by a well-meaning friend that you must take the Band-Aid off when you take a bath and clean out the cut. You deny that it is worse and continue to wear the Band-Aid. You are motivated to keep the Band-Aid on because you so fear the pain of the water on the sore. If you convince yourself that the cut is okay, you can prolong the pain of the cleaning.

What does this have to do with immorality?

Immorality is to the believer what ice cream is to the little boy and what the Band-Aid is to the wounded person. It is one of the wrong solutions to unaddressed problems or unmet needs.

There are certainly other wrong solutions—overeating, drugs, alcohol—but sexual immorality is a strong enticement when the problem area involves relationships. It is important to recognize the master tempter in this scenario. Satan pulls out all the stops in attempting to disable Christians. Because we know that God does not tempt us to sin, we need to watch out when a particularly alluring person crosses our path at a time when we least expect it.

When problems and needs are acknowledged, then they can be worked out in a godly way. When unacknowledged, Satan may put a big dish of ice cream in front of you instead of the spinach you need. He will entice you with what he knows you'll respond to.

Denial may allow a person to go for a long time making it look like everything is fine, in complete order. Some people may live an entire lifetime in an ongoing state of denial. They may never admit the truth, and they may never fall into sexual immorality. But—they will miss the life the Lord intends His people to live, and they will be in the precarious position of having the denied area of their lives open to wrong solutions.

We read the observation of God in Jeremiah 8:11-12:

> "They dress the wound of my people as though it were not serious. 'Peace, peace,' they say, when there is no peace. Are they ashamed of their loathsome conduct? No, they have no shame at all; they do not even know how to blush. So they will fall among the fallen; they will be brought down when they are punished."

The leaders of the people of Israel were claiming that things were not as they really were. That situation was probably more obvious than a problem in a marriage. But the results may be the same: denying lack of peace but falling into "loathsome conduct" as an answer.

Taking an honest look

Most people sense to some degree when they have a problem. From all outward appearances, they may seem to be completely oblivious. But inside, we all have some flicker of awareness when things in our lives are not as God intends. The pain of facing denied issues may be great. There may be strong motivation to continue to ignore the pain and the issues themselves. But the longer denial goes unanswered, the greater the possibility for harmful results.

When immorality is the result, it is only a temporary "solution." How often have you seen a couple divorce, remarry, divorce again—and on and on? The problem was never the love of one person replacing another. It was a deeper issue that was never properly addressed and worked out.

When a Christian denies that sexual immorality is wrong, there is a breakdown in thinking. The Bible makes it clear that immorality is a sin. To deny it is to lie to yourself and to others. As Christians, we simply cannot compartmentalize our thinking to accommodate a particular sin. If we say we are believers, certain actions or a desire for certain actions will follow. Attempts may be made to justify immorality by saying that God understands and will forgive. But to deny that immorality is wrong and to continue in that direction is not biblical. The ramifications of that kind of thinking are still to be seen in the lives of many professing Christians.

When true repentance occurs and lifestyles change, God can do marvelous works of restoration. Denying sin, however, is not a characteristic of a repentant heart.

Getting rid of denial

If you recognize denial as a part of your own life, then consider taking the following steps.

- Admit the truth. Whatever it may be, just admit it to yourself.
- Risk admitting the truth to your spouse or the person you are involved with.
- Be willing to live with some pain as you go through the process of working out unresolved issues.
- Determine to live by biblical standards—no matter what happens.
- Replace denial with God's perspective of your problems or needs.
- Seek help, if needed, to determine God's perspective.
- Recognize that your problems and needs can be met in a godly way.

FOUR

Unfulfilled Expectations

Ron assumed a nonchalant attitude as he dressed for his class reunion. He and Mary had arrived on an afternoon flight and checked into the hotel with just enough time left to change for the evening. It seemed strange to be in a hotel in your hometown. All of Ron's family had moved away, and he didn't want to stay at the home of one of his old friends. He didn't admit that the hotel scene better fit the image he wanted to project—but it did.

"Twenty years," he thought as he checked his image in the mirror. "Twenty years ago I was voted most athletic, most versatile, and most ambitious." He had dated the "most attractive" girl in the class, Nancy, but he had ended that romance when he left for college and a bright future. He glanced past his own image in the mirror toward his wife of eleven years. Mary was steady, faithful, and gave a nice appearance. She wasn't the cutest girl in her high school class, but she was a good choice.

Ron had accepted Christ while in college. Eventually he and Mary were married and established a home based on biblical principles. They had two children, and Ron was an executive with a major manufacturing company. Life had been good to them. Ron's mental evaluation stopped as he made his last mirror check.

As they approached the entrance to the grand ballroom, Ron felt a lump in his throat and his hands began to sweat. The grand ballroom—the scene of the high school prom. He and Nancy had been the couple of the evening. He was the envy of every guy there.

Nancy was the picture of Sandra Dee and Annette Funicello all wrapped up into one package. Ron had been the jock with looks, personality, and a star-studded future.

"What happened?"

The question entered his mind by surprise. "What happened?" he thought. "Why, nothing *wrong* happened. I *am* a success. I have a great job, a great family. Everything is fine." He drifted mentally to something he had read once in a Hemingway novel: "Like looking with your eyes at something, say a passing coast line, and then looking at it with 15 X binoculars. Or rather, maybe, looking at it and then going in and living in it—and then coming out and looking at it again."[2]

The dryness in Ron's throat increased as he realized that the living of his life had not been what it looked like it would be twenty years ago. Twenty years ago the "passing coast" looked lush and abundantly beautiful. Now, living on the shore, it had its share of weeds and polluted water. As he pulled back to look at it on this evening of nostalgia, his perception had certainly changed from that of a high-riding high school senior.

Nothing was *wrong,* but it certainly was different. He had not become what he had anticipated becoming. His expectation of life was to be the best, the brightest, the most successful—just like he had been in high school.

His thoughts were mercifully interrupted by the overly friendly voice behind the reception table. "Ronnn!" she squealed. "Why, you haven't changed a *bit*!"

"You must have," he thought, unable to remember this person from his past. He was rescued when an old girlfriend of the girl-from-behind-the-desk appeared and they giggled off together with shrieks of laughter.

He was relieved to find people he *did* remember. Ron and Mary sat at a table of former jocks and their wives and relived the glory days with great gusto. The "memory time" began with slides of those good old days. Ron was enjoying the show as he watched his successes brought back to center stage. The lights came up and everyone applauded vigorously.

"What are you doing now?" someone strangely familiar asked from behind him.

He turned his head and felt the blush immediately. Nancy was looking better than ever, smiling down at him. She was alone so he asked her to join Mary and himself. Ron felt terribly uncomfortable as he tried to make his rather ordinary life sound exciting. The evening went downhill from there. He heard about Nancy's disappointment when her marriage ended in divorce two years ago. He talked to other past-heroes and heard their tales of woe or their exaggerated tales of success.

Later that night, back in the hotel room, he felt a heaviness, a sadness he couldn't express. Mary left him to his own thoughts, trying to empathize with his pain as he looked at his life in terms of what he once thought it would be when hopes and dreams were all that lay ahead.

In the weeks that followed, Ron began to admit that his life had not turned out as he had originally hoped. It was okay, but it was not what he had expected. He slipped into an attitude of self-pity and discouragement. Mary tried to encourage him, but nothing helped. He became angry and irritable. Comparison became part of his everyday focus.

His thoughts were so out of focus that when the phone call from Nancy came, he was completely unprepared. She was going to be in town on business. Could they have lunch? That was the beginning. Nancy got the job she was interviewing for and moved within miles of Ron's home.

They were only friends, he told himself. And that's what he told Mary, and anyone else who would ask. Just old high school friends. But Nancy made him feel young again. She reminded him of the times when he *was* a big deal. He reveled in her adoration. He began to live a fantasy where past and present got mixed up. He couldn't go back and live the last twenty years over again, but he could recapture the *feelings* of that time for brief moments when he was with Nancy in the present.

His affair almost cost him his marriage. It *did* cost him any chance for a friendship with Nancy. Ron's problem was that he handled unfulfilled expectations in a naive, damaging way. He grasped at something ungodly that made him feel the way he felt back when the expectations were all ahead of him. He paid a heavy price for a few moments of relived glory.

Unfulfilled expectations may bring out an "I have a *right*-to" attitude.

To "expect" is to consider something probable, or perhaps even certain, necessary, or "owed" to us. What happens when we consider something to be owed to us and we don't get it? Chances are that our first reaction is anger, disillusionment, a sense of being unfairly treated. Many of the "diseases of the attitude" (discussed in Chapter 6) come into play. Our pride is hurt, we feel ungrateful. Of course, none of these are biblical responses, but they are all common ones. Think of how the Lord must feel when we respond badly to what He *has* given us by complaining about what we do *not* have.

We who are parents may experience that disappointment from our own children. It seems status quo these days that a teen receives a car when he or she turns sixteen, or as a graduation present from high school. Suppose a teenage boy has hinted and hinted about the car he desires. It's new, it's a sports car, it's expensive. And he is graduating! His parents do buy him a car, but it is not-so-new, it is not a sports car, it is still expensive. There is the possibility that the teenage boy may respond in a less than totally appreciative way. Why? Because he believes that he deserves his unfulfilled expectation.

One biblical example of this is found in 2 Kings 5. Naaman, a commander in the army of the king of Aram, had leprosy. Elisha sent word to the king to have Naaman come to him because of his leprosy.

> So Naaman went with his horses and chariots and stopped at the door of Elisha's house. Elisha sent a messenger to say to him, "Go, wash yourself seven times in the Jordan, and your flesh will be restored and you will be cleansed." But Naaman went away angry and said, "I thought that he would surely come out to me and stand and call on the name of the LORD his God, wave his hand over the spot and cure me of my leprosy." (2 Kings 5:9-11)

You would think that Naaman's major concern would have been the curing of the leprosy. But he had an expectation of how that would be handled, and when it was less than he expected, he got mad. He was so mad about his unfulfilled expectation that he missed the fact that the Lord was going to cure him of his leprosy. Naaman had some servants who pointed out to him that he would have been willing to do some difficult thing to be cured, so why not go and wash in the river? He did, and was cleansed of his leprosy.

Feeling we have a "right" to something can lead to serious problems. There are many things we may *expect* over which we have little control. We may be ambitious, aggressive, determined to reach some goal—and yet the goal may slip through our fingers. There is a certain school of thought that promotes the idea that you can achieve anything you set your mind to. That is simply not always true.

You may achieve a great deal. You may even achieve a series of goals. But, when matters outside of your control enter the picture, you may lose the ability to attain some specific aim. Then the feelings of unfulfilled expectations surface. Immorality may result because an immoral relationship may also be one of the most sympathetic relationships around. When a person feels cheated or let down by life, it is a great comfort to find someone who agrees with him.

Immorality often breeds partners who feed on each other's weaknesses. A woman meets a man who is feeling sorry for himself because he has not gotten what he thought he deserved out of life. She agrees with him and sets out to meet his need to feel significant. Instead of pointing out what he *does* have, she feeds his ungrateful spirit by trying to be the one person in his life who understands what he really did deserve. She will stand by him and comfort him in this unfair world. He, in turn, will allow her to need to be needed (she may have expected to be a Florence Nightingale nursing someone to health, but ended up with a healthy partner), but they will only serve to promote weaknesses in each other.

What about God's perspective?

If we have a relationship with Jesus Christ and believe the Bible to be the Word of God, then we have no room for wallowing in the swamp of self-pity. If we don't have what we previously expected, then God apparently did not intend us to have it. This premise is based on the assumption that we have not been disobedient to the Lord. If we are unfaithful, and, as a result, suffer the consequences of that unfaithfulness, then we are reaping what we have sown.

For instance, if a person commits adultery and ends up in a divorce, he or she cannot say that God intended that marriage to fail.

The failure may be the consequence of an unbiblical action. But—if we have attempted to follow the Lord and still do not have what we thought we would have, then God did not intend it. Jeremiah 29:11 is the classic verse for this thought: "'I know the plans I have for you,' declares the LORD, 'plans to prosper you and not to harm you, plans to give you hope and a future.'"

You may be reading this and saying, "I have tried to walk with the Lord. But my life hasn't turned out the way I expected. It also doesn't seem to be prosperous, harmless, and hopeful." This is a tough situation to answer in human terms. Many of our lives are full of pain and disappointment—and yet we are to believe that God has a plan that is good. It may require a great deal of faith to believe that. Part of what we need to do is to take ourselves out of the element of time and give God room to work. We cannot see the end. We cannot see how a particular thread of pain in our lives is weaving a greater purpose. Sometimes the greater purpose doesn't seem worth the pain of the sewing of that particular thread.

We often expect relief or answers from God by a certain time. When the relief or the answer doesn't come, we don't *feel* that He has a very good plan. In those moments, the only option is to go on in obedience. That sounds so harsh and insensitive. But, that is what we are called to do.

Abraham probably wondered about the goodness of God's plan for him to be the father of many nations when he was an old man and still had no children. Moses probably wondered about his life purpose when he spent forty years tending flocks before he was called to lead the Israelites out of Egypt. Joshua probably wondered on the fourth time around Jericho just what the Lord had in mind.

Your life and my life may not turn out like those of Abraham, Moses, or Joshua. But God does have a plan for each one of us. We may never know this side of heaven just what purpose God is accomplishing. But that is not for us to determine. We are to determine to trust Him and be obedient.

In the middle of a life of unfulfilled expectations, one thing we are *not* to do is to choose any ungodly course. Immorality is not justified even when circumstances are tough and when sympathy, or even love, is offered by someone who has no right before the Lord to offer it.

Our expectations are in God.
Andrew Murray says in "The Believer's Secret to Waiting on God" that "waiting on God becomes [our] brightest hope and joy."[3] He goes on to say that the reason we can do this is that we are waiting on *God.* *What* we are waiting for is nothing compared to *who* we wait for. We can have hope when we switch our expectations from specific circumstances to God Himself.

To do this, it is absolutely essential that we develop a long-term view of life. If we cannot learn to trust beyond a particular circumstance, we will have no lasting peace in this world. (Chapter 26 deals with the importance of an eternal perspective.)

Immorality produces real shortsightedness. The next encounter is about as far as the participants see. Because meetings are usually secret, they may not be able to be planned much in advance. This "cloak and dagger" atmosphere adds to the excitement of the involvement. Lifting one's perspective to the long-range purposes of God are tough to accomplish from that low-lying vantage point.

Perspective comes with time and understanding. For now, it is important to accept that God's plan is good, regardless of how many unfulfilled expectations are in your life.

What to do
Let's go back to Hemingway's illustration: "Like looking with your eyes at something, say a passing coast line, and then looking at it with 15 X binoculars. Or rather, maybe, looking at it and then going in and living in it—and then coming out and looking at it again."

Once you looked at the coastline of your future life from afar. It looked perfect. You approached the coastline and lived there a while. Things did not turn out to be as you thought when you were looking at it from a distance. Marriage wasn't quite as you imagined. Work certainly wasn't. There were many good times. But tough ones, too. You never saw even a hint of the tough ones from the distance.

Now you have rowed out from the shore for a moment and are looking back at it. You now wonder how you could have perceived it so incorrectly long ago.

Now what?

You have to go back. It is your life. You cannot just watch it like a spectator at a football game. This is the one you play.

You can go back and dream about what it did not turn out to be.

Or, you can go back and begin to see what God intends for you to do with your particular part of the coastline.

One thing you don't want to do is to go back and make a mess of what is there. If you go back into your life and handle it with ungodliness, you will destroy what is there.

FIVE

Emotional Pain

Fran knew that the image she projected was one of confidence. That wasn't a false image. It just wasn't the whole picture.

"But," she would reason to herself, "why should I 'air my dirty laundry' for all the world to see?"

She moved about her world in the light of day with a smile.

At night—alone—she anguished. She was unable to hide her loneliness in the dark. The light offered so many activities and pretenses of fulfillment. But, in the night, there was nothing. Nothing but the pain.

Fran had been a Christian almost all her life. She was raised in a church and had accepted Christ as a child. Her family was loving and she had as close a relationship as geographical distance would allow. Fran had been offered a "golden" job with a Christian organization. It involved a move away from home, which she decided would be good for her. She was in her mid-thirties, unmarried and flexible. The move had been a relatively smooth one. Her coworkers took her along with them to church until she found one she was comfortable with. Fran immediately got involved and seemed "happy" with her new life.

That had been four years ago. They had not been bad years. But they had been lonely. It seemed difficult to establish deep friendships—and she was so busy being successful. She had dated only casually and occasionally. Her moral stand was impeccable.

But, the nights. They were really getting tough. So alone.

Fran met Ed at work. He had transferred in from another location and was in the process of getting established. Since Fran knew that whole "newcomer routine," she offered to show Ed around. They would not have described their relationship as one of "dating." But, they were spending a lot of time together. Ed was divorced, a Christian, alone.

They developed an intimate friendship that led, in a matter of weeks, to an affair. Fran suffered tremendous guilt over her actions. She kept intending to end it. But, she was no longer alone in the dark.

When self-esteem is damaged

Gill had been in the pastorate for about ten years. He started a church that grew steadily over those years. In terms of ministry, he was certainly considered successful. His wife was active in the church's work, and all seemed well. Gill's denomination supported a proposal by his church to have a group break off and start a sister church on the other side of town. Gill was in agreement and helped with the beginning steps of that process.

The new pastor called to plant the sister church was dynamic and effective in the pulpit. Gill's congregation was excited about what this church, and this new man, could offer. Soon, some of the old, regular attenders of Gill's church started to visit the new one. Gill understood their curiosity and was not alarmed.

Not at first.

Attendance at Gill's church started to drop off. It took two years for Gill to face what had happened. He was still preaching. He still had a church. But it was dead. People would come and go. There were a few faithful diehards. But it had slipped from his grasp. Gill told himself that his significance was not wrapped up in his work. He told himself that, but he did not really believe it.

His self-esteem was badly damaged.

There was a young woman he was counseling in his congregation. She became as good a listener for him as he was for her. The affair that began by making him feel better about himself only served to further tear down his already crumbling life.

Causes of emotional pain

"Three primary sources of emotional pain are: 1. lack of self-worth, 2. lack of intimacy with others, or loneliness, 3. lack of intimacy with

God."[4] I believe another significant source is that of loss.

In the previous illustrations, Fran was suffering from a lack of intimacy with others and Gill was suffering from a lack of self-worth. They both lacked true intimacy with God. The results of such pain can often drive us to great lengths to find relief.

Lack of intimacy with others may be a need that goes unnoticed for quite some time. We can easily fool ourselves to believe that we are satisfied, even without close relationships, by gratification from work, church obligations, and other superficial activities. Because that need for personal intimacy is in us and growing, when it does surface, it can be explosive. The level of pain experienced when we face true loneliness can be very intense. If we are caught by surprise by this pain, there is an equal amount of intensity pressuring us to relieve it.

Lack of self-worth is a fertile field for immorality to take root. If we are feeling bad about ourselves, and a person comes along who is not only sympathetic but builds up our damaged ego, look out. It is only natural to be drawn to warm and caring compliments. These compliments are not an authentic measure of our self-worth, but we are unable to evaluate that truth in light of our pain. All we know is that we feel bad and that being with this certain person makes us feel good. (Authentic self-worth is discussed in Chapter 27.)

Lack of intimacy with God is difficult to determine. Our world relates "intimacy" with sexual encounter so closely that our thinking is nebulous when defining a relationship with God that is intimate. (True intimacy with God is discussed in Chapter 8.)

The pain of loss

Emotional pain caused by loss can also be devastating. The loss may be as dramatic as the death of a loved one or as inevitable as the loss of youth. Life is a series of losses. We may often feel we are prepared for them, but the reality is difficult to live with.

My older daughter graduated from high school this year and is planning to go to college in the fall. I have anticipated the coming of this time for the past eighteen years. It is still very difficult. I am thrilled for her, excited about what the Lord will do in her life, and looking forward to a new dynamic with my younger daughter. But, there is pain. It is not a situation I would choose to change. I would not like to see her sit home with me and keep me company. I want her to go on with her life. But, there is still pain. It is the pain of loss. It is a natural loss created by the passing of time.

Looking for relief

Emotional pain resulting from loss needs to be recognized and faced. We can attempt to make changes to disguise the loss—as in the case of aging, when we cover, tuck, and camouflage the signs of physical atrophy—but the loss is still real. How often do we hear about immorality entering a man's life because of a "mid-life crisis"? A mid-life crisis is the harsh reckoning with the loss of youth.

We may not all suffer greatly from lack of self-worth or lack of intimacy, but we will all suffer losses. The way we handle all these losses may sometimes be incorrect. There are both correct and incorrect ways. But sometimes we lose sight of the difference because our primary focus is just getting rid of the pain.

Anyone who has suffered great physical pain knows the driving attempt to ease that pain. We go to doctors, take medication, and undergo surgery. The pain resulting from the surgery is often intense, but worth the effort if relief is the end result. The beginning of the end of physical pain is for a doctor to diagnose what is causing that pain. He carefully examines the patient. If the cause is not obvious, he will run tests. Once he has diagnosed the cause, he prescribes a cure. If there is no cure, he attempts to ease the pain and help the patient to cope with the illness.

Diagnosis of emotional pain may be as painful a process as the experience of the pain itself. Low self-esteem, loneliness, lack of intimacy with God, and personal loss are not easy issues to face. If we can take the pills of busyness or denial, perhaps we can avoid surgery. And, if those fail, there might be comfort in a relationship with another person.

How does immorality slip into a person's life who is experiencing great emotional pain? It does so in the form of relief. The adversary disguises it to look good and justified in the early stages. By the time it is seen as bad medicine, it is well into the system of the patient.

Emotional pain dramatically blurs our vision.

In the middle of deep emotional pain, immorality can be rationalized and appear justified because our vision is blurred. We are viewing life through the eyes of one focused on relief, not on the Lord. Temptation is heightened because we can actually experience little tastes of relief in the early stages of a relationship with a sympathetic person.

I hate to bring up the word "patience." It is one of my least favorite areas of growth. I do not like to wait. I want to solve issues *now.* If it is a painful issue, I want to solve it *before* now. Solving something now often results in solving it incorrectly. How often we can look back at a decision made in the middle of great pain and wonder how we ever arrived at such a decision. Patience to live in the middle of pain is a valued commodity for the believer.

Of course, the most familiar biblical example of patience is Job. He had a first-class case of pain and the need for patience. He was incapacitated to the point that physical behavior was limited, but we are allowed to see into the recesses of his thinking and identify with the mental turmoil he endured. Job's temptation was not one of immorality, but he did succumb to another temptation in the midst of his trouble. He challenged God. God met that challenge in a confrontation with Job on exactly who Job was in relation to Him. Job acknowledged that humbling reality and, in the end, God richly blessed him.

For us, our particular sufferings and temptations may be different than Job's, but the principle is the same: When we try to find relief in ways that are not biblical, we will inevitably fail to attain that relief. Emotional pain is a terrible thing to endure, but the solution is not anything unbiblical.

When we are in terrible pain, we think that no one could possibly ever endure the level of torment we are experiencing. Sometimes we rationalize that this degree of pain warrants an unbiblical response. I know that in my own life the recurrence of old hurts sometimes surprises me and makes me feel sorry for myself. Just this past year, after a particularly painful night, I wrote the following notes in a journal. I realized a new level of acceptance on my part for the pain that is a part of my life. The words in quotes come from an old torch song that comes back to me in times of nostalgia.

What'll I Do?

"What'll I do when you are far away, and I am blue, what'll I do?"

Long ago and far away there was a man I loved. I loved him, married him, bore his children, and buried him. He left my life suddenly, unexpectedly—accidentally. A fatal accident.

And, now, he's far away. And I get blue. What do I do? Even after all these years? There are moments of such intense pain that I scream in my soul for relief. I lay in my bed in the depths of darkness and anguish there. Heaviness pushes in on me so that my chest seems to be under me pressing up against my back to escape. There is nothing of me that is not wracked with pain—my body, my thoughts, my memory, my dreams—everything.

We wrestle—pain and I. I break pain's hold for a moment. A verse, a prayer, a thought of Jesus, and I elude pain—for a moment. Then the wave returns. It washes over my comfort with renewed force, and I hurt again.

"What'll I do when you are far away, and I am blue, what'll I do?"

What do I do? I hurt. Again.

After fighting until near exhaustion, I rest. Stillness. The pain is still in me. I feel it intensely. But, now—I hold it instead of it holding me. I hold it and wring out of it every drop of bitter potion I can extract. It drips into every pore of me. Nothing is left protected. All areas of my life and thought and being experience the full impact of pain.

And, fear is gone. There is nothing left to hurt. I am exposed, an open wound with salt sprinkled throughout. I don't try to escape. I don't reason with pain. I accept it.

Pain hurts beyond the ability of words to describe. But, life without pain is death—death to risk or joy or caring deeply. If there had been no man I had loved deeply, I would not hurt so badly at the remembrance of his loss.

"When I'm alone with only dreams of you—that won't come true, what'll I do?"

I will hurt, wrestle, rest, hold on, accept, and hurt again.

Pain is still part of my life. The way I handle it is not to look for relief in unbiblical ways.

The rest of this book deals with what the biblical answer is. If low self-esteem, lack of intimacy with others and with God, and a deep sense of loss are part of your life, there is a way to handle them that is honoring to the Lord.

It is not easy.

It is not a list of things to do.

It is a process.

Pain will still be a part of your life, but an authentic relationship with Jesus Christ can drastically alter the way you are able to live with it.

SIX

Diseases of the Attitude

"He has such a bad attitude!"

That's the way people who knew Jim described him.

"One day he's bored, the next he's bragging about how great he is. He's selfish and complaining. His jealousy is blatant, and his ungrateful spirit is disgusting."

This Jim sounds like a little too much to bear. But we all know people who have attitude problems that come out in a variety of ways. People who suffer from diseases of attitude don't take responsibility for their own actions. They blame their circumstances, other people, and even God for their "bad moods."

Because people with attitude problems lack a sense of responsibility, they are high-risk candidates for immorality. Why? Because if they feel they are not responsible, they can shift the guilt of the wrong behavior to someone or something else. They are masters at rationalization. This certainly doesn't mean that everyone with an attitude problem is committing some kind of immorality. But in looking at the causes of immorality, the "bad attitude" personality is in a posture of vulnerability.

What's in an attitude?

An attitude is a disposition of the mind or emotions. Attitudes are expressed in a number of ways: the way you say something, the expression on your face, your silence, your body language, your behavior. Your entire presence conveys an "attitude." You don't have to come right out and say what you feel. You end up communicating your pleasure or displeasure, approval or disapproval, in a dozen different ways.

A "bad" attitude is one that approaches something or someone with a perspective that is not biblical. The focus of the person with a bad attitude is on the circumstance he or she is responding to, not on the Lord.

But what does this have to do with immorality? To begin with, people with diseases of the attitude are blame shifters. They can be involved in poor behavior and not even acknowledge it because they don't take the responsibility for their own actions. Sexual immorality can be a result of looking only at the act itself and not at what the Lord says about it or your own responsibility in it.

People with attitude problems are shortsighted. They can "live for the moment" without much regard for what preceeded the moment, or what the consequences of the moment will be.

As believers, we must view the facts of life with a mental position that is in line with Scripture. If God says that immorality is wrong, then our attitude toward it should be that it is wrong. A disease of the attitude can alter a biblical evaluation of reality.

Ungratefulness

There is a well documented account of the ungratefulness of the children of Israel. In Deuteronomy 9:7 Moses says, "Remember this and never forget how you provoked the LORD your God to anger in the desert. From the day you left Egypt until you arrived here, you have been rebellious against the LORD." In Psalm 78:11 we read, "They forgot what he had done, the wonders he had shown them."

An ungrateful attitude looks at what we do not have, not at what we have had or have right now. If we are ungrateful for what the Lord has done, we may seek our own ways of gratification.

Immorality in the face of ingratitude is like a spoiled child taking what his parent has denied him. He feels he ought to be able to have it, so he takes it. He doesn't care that five chocolate bars will make him sick. He wants them. He takes them. He suffers with a stomachache later, but has no thought of it while stuffing down the candy. Filled with the wrong things, he has a continued ungrateful attitude when faced with substantial food at mealtime.

Selfishness

Because we are fallen creatures, we are all selfish. Even if we don't want to be selfish, we naturally lean that way. Paul says in Romans 7:14-16, "We know that the law is spiritual; but I am unspiritual, sold as a slave to sin. I do not understand what I do. For what I want to do I do not do, but what I hate I do."

We find our reconciliation for this sinful condition in Romans 8:1-2: "There is now no condemnation for those who are in Christ Jesus, because through Christ Jesus the law of the Spirit of life set me free from the law of sin and death." If we have the Holy Spirit and live according to the Spirit, then we can control the selfishness in us. It is still there, but it is controlled.

We often hear from people trapped in immorality that they became involved out of love. On the surface, that might sound legitimate. But true love from one believer to another would sacrifice immoral desire for the good of the other. When we are involved in immorality, we are being used as an instrument of sin in that other person's life. It is a lie of Satan that an immoral relationship is an expression of love. It may feel emotionally like love, but it is selfish.

Boredom

Hedonism is a philosophy stating that pleasure or happiness is the sole or chief good in life. We live in a truly hedonistic culture. The pursuit of pleasure has become an accepted goal of life.

Solomon made a heavy attempt at hedonism. In Ecclesiastes 2:10-11, he evaluates his pursuit:

> I denied myself nothing my eyes desired; I refused my heart no pleasure. My heart took delight in all my work, and this was the reward for all my labor. Yet when I surveyed all that my hands had done and what I had toiled to achieve, everything was meaningless, a chasing after the wind; nothing was gained under the sun.

Immorality can play either a blatant or a subtle part in the pursuit of pleasure. Believers might, for example, be pursuing pleasure in moral ways as far as their behavior, but not in their motivation. When they find that their "moral" pursuit of pleasure doesn't have long-term satisfaction, boredom may set in. The old saying goes, "An idle mind is the devil's workshop." Someone who is bored is obviously not thinking with interest about much of anything. Idleness leaves room for incorrect thinking to invade.

But an attitude of boredom is not scriptural. God declares in Jeremiah 29:11, "I know the plans I have for you . . . plans to prosper you and not to harm you, plans to give you hope and a future." Prosperous plans will not be boring. If we are caught in a state of boredom, our focus is off the Lord and His plan and on instant gratification.

As Christians we need to be concerned about things that concern the Lord. We are not to throw stones, but we are to make personal commitments to Christ and then help others to do the same.

Apathy

An apathetic person doesn't care. When we don't care, we are not motivated to protect ourselves from sin. God rebuked the church in Laodicea for their apathy: "I know your deeds, that you are neither cold nor hot. I wish you were either one or the other! So, because you are lukewarm—neither hot nor cold—I am about to spit you out of my mouth" (Revelation 3:15-16).

Now does this mean that God wants us to be cold toward Him? No. But He does want us to decide. If we are truly believers, then He wants us to take a stand about sin. He wants us to be for Him, but if we are not, to stop pretending, to stop holding on to the lukewarm trappings of Christianity and having lukewarm attitudes about sin.

If we have an "I don't get bothered too much" attitude about the state of morality in the Christian community, we may come up against a test we are not ready to face.

Jealousy

The "green-eyed monster" of jealousy has started many a flirtatious encounter. A jealous person has a tendency to lash out. In a relationship, one person often deals with hurt by dealing out a little hurt in return. Although this is obviously not the proper way to handle hurt, it happens frequently. What may start out to be simply an act to stir jealousy can end up being one of improper involvement.

Saul's jealousy of David drove him to try to murder him. It was to be a driving force for the rest of Saul's life. He inappropriately compared himself with David.

If someone we love in an exclusive way seems interested in another person, we will certainly be hurt. If we start to compare ourselves with that other person, we are way off focus. Then, if we compound the problem by attempting to cause jealousy by showing interest in yet another person, the web of turmoil becomes a tangled mess.

Hopelessness

One of Satan's greatest lies is that we have no hope. Belief in this lie can result in debilitating discouragement. And when we're discouraged, what does anything matter? We may come to feel we have nothing to lose because we have already seemingly lost everything.

Job is the classic example of someone with cause to be discouraged. He must have suffered great times of hopelessness. Chapter 30 of the book of Job is 31 verses of hopelessness. But God did not let Job go. Because He contended with him, at the end of the account Job says, "Surely I spoke of things I did not understand, things too wonderful for me to know" (Job 42:3). Job's hopelessness was replaced with double the blessing he had before his ordeal.

When we are discouraged and nothing at the moment seems to matter, something that truly matters a lot may look irrelevant. What is immorality in the face of a life in shambles for any number of reasons? Our reasoning becomes clouded with comparisons. Compared to the mess we may be in, immorality looks inconsequential. But it does matter. No matter what happens in our lives, immorality is never justified.

Pride

Pride is the prince of bad attitudes. It is often the preamble to disaster. When we are full of pride, we feel exempt. We feel above others and in total control of our lives. We read in the book of Daniel how King Nebuchadnezzar felt this same kind of consuming pride:

> As the king was walking on the roof of the royal palace of Babylon, he said, "Is not this the great Babylon I have built as the royal residence, by my mighty power and for the glory of my majesty?"

The words were still on his lips when a voice came from heaven, "This is what is decreed for you, King Nebuchadnezzar: Your royal authority has been taken from you. You will be driven away from the people and will live with the wild animals; you will eat grass like cattle. Seven times will pass by for you until you acknowledge that the Most High is sovereign over the kingdoms of men and gives them to anyone he wishes." (Daniel 4:30-32)

When we are suffering from pride, we feel we can do just about anything and get away with it. We act as if we are not under God's authority.

Immorality is just one sin that may result from any of these diseases of attitude. An important fact to realize is that an attitude problem is just a reflection of a deeper issue. If we feel hopeless, we are not viewing life scripturally. Being bored, selfish, and ungrateful is a clear-cut indication of the state of our relationship with the Lord. Since this book is dealing with immorality, we won't go into the multitude of reasons that these kinds of attitudes exist. To be aware of them is a start. To recognize that they are places of risk and vulnerability with regard to immorality is a preventive measure.

Christian businessman after involvement with coworker: "When we are vulnerable and suffering from low self-esteem and unfulfilled expectations, we try to find fulfillment in worldly things. It is important to put our focus on Christ and get our fulfillment from Him. I believe that if I had been more fastidious in prayer and willing to recognize my weakness and turn my problems over to Him—in a really sincere *way—I would never have gotten into this situation."*

Christian single woman: "I had a commitment to Christ, but it was a weak one. I felt because I was single I was missing something. I tried to live a strong commitment to Christ in other areas but was weak when it came to emotional involvement with men."

SEVEN

A Weak Commitment to Christ

Her father had been killed in World War II. She never even saw him. Gloria was born a few months after he left for the Pacific. He never came home. Her mother would sit and talk for hours about his days at the Naval Academy and later his appointment to the Pacific Fleet after the bombing of Pearl Harbor.

Gloria grew up with a legacy of understanding what commitment and honor really meant. Her mother explained that her father had made a commitment that required even his life. He had made it willingly—and the ultimate price *had* been required of him. There was a picture of her father in their den next to a framed collection of medals—colored ribbons with little insignias attached. In the bottom drawer of her mother's dresser, there was a neatly folded American flag.

Gloria had also grown up hearing about having a personal relationship with Jesus Christ. Her mother talked to her of inviting Jesus into her heart and making a commitment to Him. Gloria prayed as a little girl for Jesus to come into her heart. But she wasn't sure what the commitment to Him meant. Her mother compared it to the commitment her father had made to his country. He had died because of that commitment.

Gloria had not seen any Christians around her die because of their commitment to Jesus. As she grew up, however, she realized that a big part of that commitment meant being willing to live a certain way. Gloria accepted that commitment the same way she had been taught to accept her father's commitment. She heard phrases about "dying to self" in order to live for Christ. That was a little harder to understand, but she moved on in her willingness to live as Christ asked.

By the time Gloria was in her forties, she could look at her life with a degree of contentment. She was married, had two teenagers, and a great job. Things seemed to go along fairly well until the children went off to college. Gloria found an air of discontent start to seep into her thinking. It was nothing serious—just a restlessness. Her Christian values had been challenged ever since she had entered the working world, but she had been able to remain faithful. Now something was happening to her thinking. Her value system was constantly being attacked. She found herself asking why it *was* so important to live a totally uncompromising life.

One day after work, Gloria stopped by to see her mother. Her mother was sitting in the den doing some needlework and Gloria was restlessly shuffling around the room. She paused in front of the desk and doodled on the note pad. Her mother was saying something, but Gloria's thoughts were drifting back to the question, "Why live a godly life? What real difference does it make?"

She was staring at the wall when her mother called her out of her private world. Gloria heard her mother's voice, but her attention was fixed on the wall in front of her. Her father's medals hung in the same spot they had occupied for over forty years.

"Look at that," Gloria thought. "That's all that's left of him. A few pieces of faded ribbon and some brass." Gloria startled herself with the thought. She had never felt that way before. The thought sobered her. "All that's left of him?" she repeated the words in her mind. "If that were all that's left of him, I wouldn't be here."

She looked at her mother who sat there with her needlework. The many hours of conversation from her childhood came flooding back. She glanced back at the framed medals with tears in her eyes. Her thoughts of a moment ago were gone. She knew that her father and all that he stood for—mattered. What he had done—mattered. He had given her life, and then he had given his life.

Her commitment to Christ, which had been wavering—mattered. *He* had given her life, and then *He* had given His life. Her commitment mattered because He mattered. He was worthy of her commitment. Her father had died for a cause he believed in; Christ had died for Gloria.

She was ashamed of her thoughts of the last few months. She was grateful that they had been only thoughts, but she was sorry she had even entertained them. Her mother looked up, puzzled. Gloria smiled, hugged her mother, and went home. Nothing had happened on the outside that others could see, but a great deal happened that day on the inside of Gloria.

She looked again at the cost of commitment—all of oneself—and counted Christ worthy of that cost.

An age of weak commitment

I attended a writer's conference a few years ago. We were on a college campus and lived in the dorms for the week of the conference. One morning I was standing at one of the sinks in the bathroom that was used by women on my floor. A young woman came in, obviously disturbed. She had been crying and was now wiping her face with angry grunts.

"Are you alright?" I asked.

"My fiancé has been transferred to *Oklahoma*!" she willingly announced.

"Oh," I said with a mild degree of confusion. "I take it you don't want him to go to *Oklahoma*!"

"*No!* We want to live in New York."

"Is this a job transfer?" I asked.

"Kind of. He's in the service and he just got orders for *Oklahoma*."

"You can still go with him, can't you? I mean you *can* go to Oklahoma, can't you?"

"Well, yes, but we want to live in New York." Her frustration level was rising.

So was mine.

"How long will he be stationed in Oklahoma?" I asked, trying to sound interested but not annoyed.

"Thirteen months!"

I couldn't take it any longer. I smiled weakly and went back to my room. I felt enraged. Thirteen months in Oklahoma. My late husband had been a helicopter pilot in the Army. Seven of his classmates in flight school had been killed in Viet Nam. They were serving thirteen-month tours. I had a number of friends who got married and kissed their new husbands goodbye—to never see them again. Others waited at home in the agony of having their husbands be part of the six o'clock news. That war was brought into our homes nightly—and this girl was complaining about *Oklahoma*!

I had not even attempted to talk to her about her attitude because, at the moment, I was having enough trouble with mine. It would probably have been a lame attempt. The gulf between us in exposure and experience was enormous. In a calmer state later, I realized that she had never lived in a time of war. She had never seen a TV broadcast of Americans being killed by the hundreds every day. She had a problem with moving to Oklahoma because that was not what she *wanted* to do. And she, like most people, was used to doing what she wanted.

We live in a day of weak commitment. It's not necessary to be involved in a military conflict to understand commitment, but it is a good comparison. Even during the protest movements of the sixties, the protesters were *committed* to what they believed. I am not making a case here for taking a stand for war or against war, but just pointing out a major difference between our society today and that of the past.

My daughters and I live in Colorado Springs, right across the highway from the Air Force Academy. We have had the opportunity to get to know some of the cadets. The rules of the Academy are typical of any military institution: discipline and commitment of the highest priority. Some of the rules may seem silly in and of themselves, but they serve a purpose. That purpose is one that my daughters have found unusual. They are so unaccustomed to having to do anything just as a discipline or for the sake of commitment that they find the Academy code of rules terribly strict.

We live in an age of ease. Since we have few examples of commitment in our human relationships, how can we understand commitment to Christ?

In William MacDonald's booklet *True Discipleship,* we find a letter describing another kind of commitment:

> Many Christians felt strongly rebuked when Billy Graham first read the following letter, written by an American college stu-

dent who had been converted to communism in Mexico. The purpose of the letter was to explain to his fiancée why he must break off their engagement:

"We Communists have a high casualty rate. We're the ones who get shot and hung and lynched and tarred and feathered and jailed and slandered, and ridiculed and fired from our jobs, and in every other way made as uncomfortable as possible. A certain percentage of us get killed or imprisoned. We live in virtual poverty. We turn back to the party every penny we make above what is absolutely necessary to keep us alive. We Communists don't have the time or the money for many movies, or concerts, or T-bone steaks, or decent homes and new cars. We've been described as fanatics. We are fanatics. Our lives are dominated by one great overshadowing factor, *the struggle for world communism.*

"We Communists have a philosophy of life which no amount of money could buy. We have a cause to fight for, a definite purpose in life. We subordinate our petty, personal selves into a great movement of humanity, and if our personal lives seem hard, or our egos appear to suffer through subordination to the party, then we are adequately compensated by the thought that each of us in his small way is contributing to something new and true and better for mankind.

"There is one thing in which I am in dead earnest and that is the Communist cause. It is my life, my business, my religion, my hobby, my sweetheart, my wife and mistress, my bread and meat. I work at it in the daytime and dream of it at night. Its hold on me grows, not lessens, as time goes on. Therefore, I cannot carry on a friendship, a love affair, or even a conversation without relating it to this force which both drives and guides my life. I evaluate people, books, ideas and actions according to how they affect the Communist cause and by their attitude toward it. I've already been in jail because of my ideas and if necessary, I'm ready to go before a firing squad."[5]

That is commitment. How does our commitment to Christ compare? Does our commitment to anything other than *self* compare?

I'm not throwing stones. I am just pointing out that we live in a society that does not help us understand commitment. We live in an environment that actually detracts from developing commitment. Of course there are professions and ministries that require a high level of commitment. But the general attitude of the day is one of "do your own thing."

Why are Americans such avid sports fans? I am one myself, so I have thought about this often. I *love* basketball. I don't play it, but I love being an avid fan. The word "fan" comes from the word "fanatic." Sometimes, I appear to be a fanatic about basketball. When my own children are playing, I am less than a model Christian. Referees could not tell my "depth of Christian character" by the way I yell at them when they call fouls on my daughters. And I am not alone. Just go to a professional football, basketball, or hockey game in this country. Grown men and women are absolutely absorbed in the competition.

It may be argued that the players are committed because they receive huge monetary rewards, at least on the professional level. But the fans—they pay to watch and scream and cry. Why? Where are our heroes? Where are the ticker-tape parades that welcome home those who have displayed commitment above and beyond the call of duty? In the last few decades, there have been a few: the men who walked on the moon in 1969, the returning hostages in 1980. But by and large, our heroes are few and far between. The average American is not called on to exercise great commitment.

So, we sit in athletic arenas and cheer our heroes on—men and women who have disciplined themselves to compete to the highest level of their sport. The archbishop of the athletic competition code was Vince Lombardi. He is quoted by high school coaches to the point that his expletives can be repeated by many a young athlete. They may not know the name, but they know the message. Among his most famous is, "Winning is not the most important thing; it is the only thing."

My two daughters play high school and college basketball. The older one learned early of the winning philosophy. It carried her over many a difficult mile. It is what makes athletes run when exhausted, play when defeated, and go on and on. She used to instruct her younger sister, "Don't *ever* ask a coach to take you out of a game because you are tired! You run until you drop, or don't run at all."

My younger daughter has done that. She has learned to condition herself so that she *can* run a whole game because she believes that it is a low level of commitment to not be able to.

I have tried to teach my girls that winning in life is similar to winning in the athletic arena. *Winning* is *everything if winning means choosing to always walk with the Lord.* It means choosing to have the highest possible level of commitment to Jesus Christ.

I don't consider my girls to have lost a game if the final score is in favor of the other team. They have lost if they have failed to try hard and to have the attitude the Lord wants them to have.

The biblical example of commitment

"Some time later God tested Abraham. He said to him, 'Abraham!' 'Here I am,' he replied. Then God said, 'Take your son, your only son, Isaac, whom you love, and go to the region of Moriah. Sacrifice him there as a burnt offering on one of the mountains I will tell you about'" (Genesis 22:1-2).

We all know the story. Abraham did what God commanded. Imagine! What could Abraham possibly come up with, logically speaking, as to why God wanted him to do that? The reason Abraham did what God commanded was that he was committed totally to God. He did not rationalize about what was good for him, but honored his commitment. I am sure he did it agonizing all the way. He must have wondered what God was doing. But he honored his commitment—even at the expense of his son's life. God delivered Isaac at the last minute. But the result in Abraham's life was abundant blessing from God: "I will surely bless you and make your descendants as numerous as the stars in the sky and as the sand on the seashore" (Genesis 22:17).

What about immorality?

Commitment to Jesus Christ is weak in our lives whenever we want to hold on to something ourselves. We may want control, some right, some way to assure that our lives will work out the way we want.

If our commitment is weak, we can rationalize immorality because we feel we have a right to some "happiness," or because we couldn't help ourselves, or because the way our lives turned out didn't make sense, so we'll change it on our own.

But strong commitment leads us to proclaim, "God says that I should be moral, and that's enough for me. I can honor that request because I honor my total commitment to the Lord."

If we withhold our commitment to the Lord in one area, we weaken all areas. This total commitment is well illustrated in the booklet *My Heart—Christ's Home* by Robert Munger. In the illustration, the Lord is occupying the heart of the believer and is comparing aspects of the heart to the rooms of a house. This area deals with the "hall closet."

> There's one more matter of crucial consequence I would like to share with you. One day I found him waiting for me at the front door. An arresting look was in his eye. As I entered, he said to me, "There's a peculiar odor in the house. Something must be dead around here. It's upstairs. I think it is in the hall closet."
>
> As soon as he said this I knew what he was talking about. Indeed there was a small closet up there on the hall landing, just a few feet square. In that closet behind lock and key I had one or two little personal things I did not want anybody to know about. Certainly I did not want Christ to see them. They were dead and rotting things left over from the old life—not wicked, but not right and good to have in a Christian life. Yet I loved them. I wanted them so much for myself I was really afraid to admit they were there. Reluctantly, I went up the stairs with him and as we mounted, the odor became stronger and stronger. He pointed at the door and said, "It's in there! Some dead thing!"
>
> It made me angry! That's the only way I can put it. I had given him access to the study, the dinning room, the living room, the workroom, the rec room, the bedroom and now he was asking me about a little two-by-four closet. I said to myself, "This is too much! I am not going to give him the key."
>
> "Well," he responded, reading my thoughts, "if you think I am going to stay up here on the second floor with this smell, you are mistaken. I will take my bed out on the back porch or somewhere else. I'm certainly not going to stay around that." And I saw him start down the stairs.
>
> When you have come to know and love Jesus Christ, one of the worst things that can happen is to sense him withdrawing

> his face and fellowship. I had to give in. "I'll give you the key," I said sadly, "but you'll have to open the closet and clean it out. I haven't the strength to do it."
>
> "I know," he said. "I know you haven't. Just give me the key. Just authorize me to handle that closet and I will." So, with trembling fingers, I passed the key over to him. He took it from my hand, walked over to the door and opened it, entered it, took out the putrefying stuff that was rotting there and threw it all away. Then he cleansed the closet, painted it and fixed it up all in a moment's time. Immediately a fresh, fragrant breeze swept through the house. The whole atmosphere changed. What release and victory to have that dead thing out of my life! No matter what sin or what pain there might be in my past, Jesus is ready to forgive, to heal, and to make whole.[6]

In giving Christ every area of our lives, we agree to live by His commandments. That includes the commandment to be pure morally. Committing to live on a higher level because He is worthy of such commitment rids us of the need to rationalize, justify, and compromise. We are free to live abundant lives based on a committed relationship with Jesus Christ.

EIGHT
The Root Cause of Immorality

Eric shut off the light and tried to go to sleep. The words stuck in his mind. His restlessness finally provoked him to get up. He quietly went downstairs and picked up the book again. It was just a novel. He had read *The Razor's Edge* by Somerset Maugham years ago, but couldn't even remember much of the story.

"His soul? It may be that he's a little frightened of himself. It may be that he has no confidence in the authenticity of the vision that he dimly perceives in his mind's eye."[7]

Eric couldn't even put the quote in with the context of the story. It glared out at him standing alone. His soul—no confidence—authenticity—vision. None of it made sense. But it bothered him greatly. He finally went back to bed and had a fitful sleep the rest of the night.

Eric was a success. He knew it, and his friends and family knew it. He was successful in business, had a beautiful home, traveled, had smart children, and had a wife who was an impeccable hostess. He was forty-five and had done it all. He was discontent. His doctor had diagnosed him as having a "mid-life crisis." Eric dismissed that notion. He knew that whatever was troubling him was a lot more than a mid-life emotional trauma.

Something deep inside of him felt empty. He had filled his life with all the possible pursuits and pleasures that man can enjoy. They had been fun and provided an exciting life. But, this yearning continued to grow. New toys and playmates would temporarily entertain him—but the emptiness would return. He often felt alone in the middle of a crowd. Always the center of attention, he never lacked for an audience. But there was no depth. Deep inside he felt alone. Utterly alone.

Eric had had times of temporary satisfaction. He always felt fulfilled and hopeful right after a new business success. He also felt confident and in control of himself and others when he would pursue a liaison with a woman—and succeed, only to end it shortly thereafter and move on to another one.

But none of the contentment of his "success" would stay. As the quote from *The Razor's Edge* said, he had no confidence in the authenticity of the vision that he dimly perceived—of himself.

No one else knew of his struggle. That kind of admission would not be consistent with the image he projected. So, he went along pretending to be on top of the world. Eric was not a religious man. He felt that religion was for weaklings. His family attended church sporadically, but it was a social function to him.

In the quiet darkness of the middle of the night, however, thoughts of the end of his life invaded his walled thinking. He could push them out in the daylight, but sometimes, at night, he could not escape. "Is that all there is?" The familiar words haunted him. Is this it? Is this day, like all the others, just a string of events and then—the end?

Eric's problem

Eric's immorality was only a reflection of a much deeper problem. His workable facade had begun to break down. What had once provided meaning in his life was no longer fulfilling. He had spent years looking for—and, to a degree, finding—significance and security in the things of this world. But the things of this world are, at best, temporary. Even if they work to make us feel good while we're alive, they end when we die.

Psychologist Larry Crabb defines security and significance this way:

> *Security:* A convinced awareness of being unconditionally and totally loved without needing to change in order to win love, loved by a love that is freely given, that cannot be earned and therefore cannot be lost.

> *Significance:* A realization that I am engaged in a responsibility or job that is truly important, whose results will not evaporate with time but will last through eternity, that fundamentally involves having a meaningful impact on another person, a job for which I am completely adequate.[8]

There is only one way that a person can truly experience lasting security and significance: in an authentic relationship with Jesus Christ. Temporary feelings of security and significance can be experienced in a number of other ways, but they all break down in the end.

All the possible causes of immorality—vulnerability, denial, emotional pain, etc.—really exist because in the midst of these risky places, we seek comfort and meaning apart from the Lord. We may be committed Christians who are trying to live as Christ would want, but we slip because we are functioning on a lie. That lie is, "The answer to my problem [whatever it may be] lies in anything other than my relationship with Christ." Now, it is true that Christ will use others in our lives to work out our problems. He will bring others alongside us to bring comfort and relief. He *never* does that in an immoral fashion. He does not justify immorality in any instance. He uses others in relationship with us, based on our relationship with Him.

The wall

When we accept Jesus Christ as our personal Lord and Savior, there is a seed of love that is planted in our heart. The Holy Spirit comes in and dwells inside of us. This is a phenomenon that is difficult to explain, but is the experience of the one who is indwelt.

It says in Philippians 4:6-7, "Do not be anxious about anything, but in everything, by prayer and petition, with thanksgiving, present your requests to God. And the peace of God, which transcends all understanding, will guard your hearts and your minds in Christ Jesus."

Having the Holy Spirit in our hearts allows us to experience a lack of anxiousness. A peace that transcends all understanding means just that. It is not necessary to understand it in order to experience it.

As new believers, we revel in that warm, secure feeling of being totally accepted by the Lord and the peace that results. As time goes by, the old self and Satan and the world start to plant weeds in the garden of our hearts. That seed of love based on the truth of our relationship with Christ begins to be stifled.

Brick by brick, a wall starts to take shape around our garden of love. The first brick may be a small doubt: Is all that God says really true? Then a brick of discouragement is laid. Pride and selfishness join the bricks. The wall grows and our awareness of the seed of love in our hearts grows dim. The mortar that holds the wall together is the world in which we live. The world's attitudes and lies cement the wall of lies in place.

We often tend to go back to the old ways. We seek security and significance in the ways of the world. Our vision of ourselves is based on the world's standard of success. Like Eric, we have no confidence in the authenticity of the vision we dimly perceive. We have lost our vision that was there when we first accepted Christ.

Tearing down the wall

"I pray that out of his glorious riches he may strengthen you with power through his Spirit in your inner being, so that Christ may dwell in your hearts through faith. And I pray that you, being rooted and established in love, may have power, together with all the saints, to grasp how wide and long and high and deep is the love of Christ, and to know this love that surpasses knowledge—that you may be filled to the measure of all the fullness of God" (Ephesians 3:16-19).

If we have truly accepted Christ as our Lord and Savior, then He dwells in our hearts. It may not feel like He dwells within, but He does. Thus we have all we need for true security and significance. We may think that we need a successful job or a happy marriage. If we have Him, and we don't have "them," then we don't *need* them. We may indeed *want* them, but we don't need them. We will certainly experience pain and disappointment without some things we want, but we can be secure and significant without our wants being met.

We all need to have security and significance. And again, that can only be found in a relationship with Jesus Christ. To tear down the wall around our hearts that prevents Christ from helping us feel His presence, we must have faith in Him and in His love. Faith grows one step at a time. It is experienced by taking God at His Word and acting on that Word. It is not an intellectual experience. It is a spiritual one that is the result of thinking and behavior based on the truth of the Bible.

For example, God says that immorality is wrong. Thus, it is important to immediately end the immoral relationship. We hesitate to give up whatever makes us feel secure. But because we have faith in Him and in His Word, we end the relationship. We experience great pain, but we persevere. In time, we heal from the unhealthy relationship and experience the forgiveness of God. Peace returns. We did not experience the feeling of peace and security *before* taking the action based on our faith. The feeling did not come until some time later.

This is, of course, an oversimplified example. The truth *is* simple. We have security and significance in Christ, which we experience by acting out of obedience to Him based on faith in Him and His Word. But tearing down the wall of lies is a slow process. The first step is the realization that we can do it, and that it is worth it.

The seemingly successful life

What about the person who seems to live a successful life, unbothered by the lack of an intimate relationship with the Lord? His life is still empty. The basis of true security and significance *must* transcend death.

The philosophy of reincarnation claims to offer life after death. Some schools of thought offer "heaven" based on good works. The worst case scenario of the unbelieving world seems to be that death is simply the end—like an endless sleep.

The Christian faith professes that there *is* a life after death, a heaven, if one has truly accepted Christ—or there is a hell, if one has not. This is an unpopular doctrine. But it is biblical. If true security and significance is based on a relationship with Jesus Christ, then it goes beyond death and into eternity. If we do not have a relationship with Jesus Christ and end up in hell, then true security and significance are no longer available. We do not have an opportunity to have a relationship with Christ after death unless we are in heaven with Him.

If security and significance were to be attainable by good works that are carried beyond this life into another one—the world of reincarnation—then people might be able to function without Christ and still feel secure and significant. Reincarnation is not biblical. It is a lie. But, many people *do* feel secure and significant based on that doctrine.

Therefore, what we base our thinking on is of upmost importance. If it is the Bible, then we *must* accept Christ in order to have security and significance in this life and after death—for all eternity.

If we base our thinking on anything other than the Bible, we may *feel* secure and significant based on our works, believing that they will carry us to a greater plane of existence. These may be sincere feelings, but they are not biblical truth.

Some people will never accept the reality of Jesus Christ. They will continue in their disbelief, thinking that they can attain true fulfillment outside of Him.

Accepting Christ

I have been assuming, to this point, that the reader already has a relationship with Jesus Christ. If you are reading this and you have never entered that relationship, you need to consider it right now. The rest of this book has no basis apart from a relationship with Christ and obedience to His Word.

In accepting Christ, you are saying to God that you understand that you are not a perfect person. You understand that you will never be a perfect person. You also understand that God, who is a loving God, is also a just God. God solved the problem of His justice and our sin by sending His Son, Jesus Christ, into the world. You understand that Jesus lived a perfect life in your place and took your punishment on the Cross in your place. He was a substitute for you. Because of His payment for your sin, you are free to have an authentic relationship with God. When you leave this world, you will go to be with the Lord forever in heaven. The reason you will seek to do good works and live a godly life is out of love, not to earn something. You accept Christ into your life.

If you not only understand this intellectually but in your heart you desire to have a relationship with Christ, then you need to tell the Lord that. Ask Him to come in and change you. Thank Him for what He will do in your life and what He will enable you to do.

Perhaps you accepted Christ years ago. But maybe, in spite of that relationship, you have fallen into the world system and based your security and significance on something other than Christ. It is not too late. He will welcome you back. A relationship with God through Jesus Christ, in the power of the Holy Spirit, is the only relationship in which we can always experience total love and acceptance. God may not accept our sin, but He continues to love us. And we have the opportunity to have an impact on Him. It is an awesome thought to grasp that we can have an impact on our Creator. We can please Him, work for Him, worship Him, and relate to Him.

Nothing can separate us from the love of Christ. Nothing can offer us more complete security and significance.

How does immorality fit in?

If nothing can separate us from the love of Christ, then what does immorality do? It hinders our relationship. It causes a lack of intimacy with Christ and short-circuits blessings that may otherwise be ours. Immorality is wrong because it is against God's plan for us.

Immorality is certainly not the only way that we seek security and significance in the wrong way. There are many others. But to realize that an immoral relationship reflects a deep need in our lives is better than to rationalize it away, justify it, or simply accept it as a weakness and stop trying to change.

It is important to see that there is a biblical way to realize true fulfillment and that immorality is not that way. Read on and become aware of the process that sometimes leads to a wrong solution for a valid need.

PART III

The Process to Immorality

Christian man after involvement with counselee: "There was a process in the involvement. It was easy in the early stages to couch my interest in her in a spritual wrapper because I was her pastor. She was attractive, but not at the top of my list. But she had some sense about her that exuded some sort of feeling of sexuality and sexual interest. It is very hard for me to remember exactly how the physical attraction actually started.

"It wasn't purely a physical thing in the early stages. The physical attraction happened as a result of other things. In fact, when you read in books about the development of an ideal relationship, you read about getting to know someone on a spiritual level, then intellectual, then emotional, and finally sexual. That is really the order in which the relationship developed. The process took over four years. It would be nice if married couples would take the time to go through that process."

NINE

"It's Not Just a One-Night Stand"

The road to immorality involves a process.
People don't just fall into immorality instantly, especially not committed Christians. Remember, we are talking about committed followers of Jesus Christ. We are talking about leaders, church members, godly men and women—you and me.

False assumptions
The road to immorality involves a process, but the reality of this process is clouded because of two false assumptions about Christians and this particular sin: (1) that people in the pastorate or leadership or counseling positions are immune to succumbing to the temptation of immorality; and (2) that because I am a committed Christian, I will never fall into immorality.

Scripture warns us, "If you think you are standing firm, be careful that you don't fall! No temptation has seized you except what is common to man" (1 Corinthians 10:12-13). If you aren't careful, you will fall before you even realize that you have been caught in the insidious web of temptation.

The Christian community is shocked when a leader is caught in immorality because we forget that absolutely *anyone* can fall, and that that person can do it while having a successful preaching, teaching, or writing ministry. Leaders may go unnoticed or unchallenged longer because of the assumption that they *couldn't possibly* be involved in an immoral sin.

When we do see leaders fall, we realize the harsh reality that this sin can, and does, happen to all types of people. It is no respecter of persons.

And we shouldn't push the issue of immorality aside because *we* seem to be okay, because we feel secure in the center of an evangelical church, have daily devotions, and memorize Scripture. These things are helpful and can help add to prevention, but they are externals. The example of the broken homes of Christian leadership indicates that we can have all these right "practices," and more, yet still fall.

Immorality is a process.

Even the proverbial "one-night stand" didn't just happen in a chance meeting. A whole series of events caused that evening of sin. Without a doubt, the people involved become aware at *some point along the way* that they are being disobedient and that they are beginning to reach the point of no return. Perhaps they even try to break the bonds that grow tighter and tighter with each encounter. And all the while, one or both of them may continue to have a fruitful ministry.

People don't lead moral lives one day and have an affair the next. It may appear that way, but it is a process. The process is often overlooked because some stages are not obvious to us, the viewer, and thus they are difficult to detect. That's why it seems to happen overnight.

Any of us could be in the process right now. None of us are immune. The earlier the danger signals can be detected and responded to, the easier it is to change direction. If you love potato chips and know that you can't stop eating them until the bag is empty, you are better off to never take the first bite. Some steps on the road to immorality are not wrong in and of themselves, yet those very steps may be the first potato chip for some people.

The seriousness of immorality

Any sin infringes on the relationship of the believer and the Lord. Any sin damages the quality of life that gives abundance and fulfillment. No other sin, however, so destroys the very foundation of the Christian marriage as sexual immorality. And no other so devastates the fiber of a person's worth. Adultery nullifies trust and destroys respect and integrity. Fornication defrauds and reduces people to objects of use, not love.

Therefore, it is essential that we be especially aware of the growing phenomenon of immorality prevalent today in the Christian community. There is absolutely no legitimate justification for immorality, yet all sorts of reasons are being given as more and more Christians indulge in this sin.

Divorce, death, and no marriage at all have swelled the ranks of singles to an extremely high percentage. Singles often meet legitimate needs in illegitimate ways. While reading through the next few chapters, which describe in detail *the process that leads to immorality,* look not only at your own situation, but at those around you. Is there a woman in the office who seems especially fond of your husband? Do you have a lonely friend who is tempted to satisfy his longings in the wrong way? You may be able to help them escape from a potentially dangerous situation. And you may be able to escape from one yourself.

We all need to determine where we are in the process that leads to immorality. We have to be "gut level" honest with ourselves and with the Lord. Let's start by looking at the first step that begins the journey away from God and into sin: the thought life.

TEN

"Mind . . . Your Own Business"

Step 1: Mere thoughts

A day at the movies

Marilyn slumped comfortably in her seat at the movie theater. "Another Friday night, and here I sit alone—but at least not at home alone," she thought as she ate another handful of buttered popcorn. "It could be worse. I could be out on another blind date . . . or at a bridal shower for some sweet young thing at the office." She wasn't feeling particularly uptight or frustrated or bitter. She was resigned to her single lifestlye. And she was just passing time in a harmless way.

The lights dimmed and the main feature began. Set in a big city, the plot revolved around the male lead's climb up the corporate ladder of success. Marilyn spotted her heroine in the opening scene. She was the administrative assistant to the aspiring executive. Single, in her thirties, beautiful, sharp—a prototype that Marilyn identified with. The young executive was, of course, married, extremely handsome, success-bound, and mildly dissatisfied with his wife.

Marilyn mentally slipped into the role of the administrative assistant. In the next two hours the plot took this sharp young woman from her desk to "his" bed, much to the pleasure of the audience because, after all, the wife was a real shrew. He had made a terrible mistake in marrying her and now *needed* the support, love, and comfort that this new "she" could provide.

There are no openly offensive bedroom scenes. This is a PG movie. The closing credits roll down the screen as "he" and "she" walk blissfully along a deserted beach, happy in their justified affair and destined to a happy, successful life together. The wife? She was written out of the script after the first hour when she packed her bags and moved home to mother.

Marilyn left the theater and reentered the real world. "It was an okay movie," Marilyn thought, as she was driving home. "The guy sure was cute." She flipped on the radio and listened to a love ballad: "Slow dancing. Can I remember that? Soft music playing in the background while being with someone who thinks I'm fabulous. Can I remember that? Candlelight dinner, roses, romance. Can I remember that?"

Because there was no man in her life now, Marilyn allowed her mind to slip into a little fantasy of cherished scenes from the past when she did feel loved. In her fantasy, she substituted the movie hero for her ex-love. As the song ended, Marilyn was surprised to realize that she had switched the mental image from the movie star to her ex-love to her present boss.

She laughed and dropped the reverie. She had much to do this weekend: the usual chores and errands, then church on Sunday morning and Bible study Sunday evening.

Monday morning at the office was typical. The phone started ringing, a mound of mail needed to be opened and processed, and two important clients were scheduled to see John, her boss, who would not be in until 10 a.m. Marilyn worked hard to get everything organized before John arrived.

He arrived promptly at ten o'clock. "Hi, Marilyn. Have a good weekend?"

Marilyn looked up from her typewriter and felt a warm blush creep up her neck and face. "Hi, John. It was okay. The usual." He walked past and into his office. Marilyn laughed at herself again because of her inner response to her very-married boss.

Driving home that night Marilyn reviewed the day. She remembered her warm glow when John first came in. She thought about him. "Wonder what he *really* thinks of me? Wonder if he's *really* happy with his wife? Wonder what it would be like to *be* with him?" Wonder, wonder, wonder.

Those "innocent" magazine ads

Patty sat down for an uninterrupted cup of coffee now that the kids were off to school. She picked up a magazine to look for new recipes.

Finding a tantalizing picture of frosted marble cake, Patty jotted down the ingredients to pick up at the store later that day.

She turned the page and saw a full-page ad for men's underwear—not a very provocative item for a housewife who has to wash these same items for her husband every week. Her eyes lingered for a moment. The man in the ad was muscular and extremely handsome. He was leaning over an equally attractive woman, who was reclining on a sofa. Though the ad was for underwear, the picture suggested much more. Putting down the magazine, Patty went upstairs to get dressed for the errand-filled day ahead.

Her husband, Scott, had been out of town for three days. He would return tomorrow. Patty was accustomed to his frequent business trips. He worked for a Christian organization, and a necessary drawback of his position was extensive travel. Their marriage of eleven years was good and solid, what you'd expect of a godly couple.

As Patty was leaving, the carpenter arrived. "Hi, Mrs. Anderson. I'll just let myself in and get to work." He was remodeling the den.

"Okay, Todd. I'll be back soon," Patty replied.

"He really has a good build," she thought as she drove away. "Kind of looks like the guy in the underwear ad."

Two hours later, Patty returned with a load of groceries. Todd came out to help her. They had a pleasant, but superficial conversation; then he returned to his work in the den.

That afternoon while waiting at school for the children, Patty pictured Todd carrying the groceries. The muscles in his back rippled. "Good grief," she thought, "What am I doing? Todd is a kid compared to me. Scott looked that good when he was younger. Wonder if Todd has a girlfriend? Wonder what she looks like? Wonder what he thinks of me?" Wonder, wonder, wonder.

If we are really honest, most of us would have to admit that we do run such scenes through our mental video—and many others that would be far more embarrassing if revealed. Though often harmless, such thinking could lead to a wrong outcome if the right opportunity were to coincide with strong, previously conceived desires.

Those dangerous mental images

Potiphar's wife probably had fantasized about Joseph many times before she invited him to bed. The story in Genesis says, "Now Joseph was well-built and handsome, and after a while his master's wife took notice of Joseph and said, 'Come to bed with me!'" (Genesis 39:6-7). It's doubtful that she noticed him one minute and invited him to bed the next. Her thinking and noticing and wondering was all part of a process that occurred over a period of time. Because she wasn't a committed believer, she had no qualms about pursuing her fantasy. But as believers, what do we do with our fantasies?

What about thoughts that do reoccur? Sometimes they make us uncomfortable because of the desires they awaken in us. And, sometimes, they lead to action that *is* harmful to ourselves and others. In this chapter, we aren't going to discuss actions. Here we are concerned with the first part of the process that can lead to immorality. Each one of us must sincerely ask the question, "What goes on in my mind?"

Romans 12:2 says, "Do not conform any longer to the pattern of this world, but be transformed by the renewing of your mind." It's getting tougher and tougher to have a Romans 12 mind-set when we live in a Romans 1 world: "God . . . gave them over to a depraved mind, to do what ought not to be done. They have become filled with every kind of wickedness, evil, greed and depravity" (1:28-29).

Ads have changed from fully-clothed, rugged cowboys riding across the range to the undressed, sensual young man lying practically on top of the young woman on the sofa. The cowboy used to advertise cigarettes on TV, but those kinds of ads have been banned from TV because of the harmful effects of smoking. The other young man, with very little pressure from the censors, advertises underwear and is highly suggestive of a lifestyle that is much more harmful than smoking!

One night I was watching a "police show" with my teenage daughter. It was the typical chase-and-catch-the-crook plot. A romance developed between the star and guest star. One love scene seemed to last an eternity. Wanting to be mature in front of my teenager, I kept quiet when the scene started with them kissing. As the action heated up, my daughter and I both became uncomfortable. We turned off the TV. And that was prime time on a major channel!

In the past, movies and ads would have given a more ideal view of marriage, family, and morality. The heroes of yesteryear were honorable. Advertisements were aimed at the married couple living in suburbia. Wholesome music was the background for people falling in love and getting married. Remember the old song lyrics, "Love and marriage . . . go together like a horse and carriage"?

One day I was singing the words to a new, catchy song I had heard. I was singing, "dancing in the streets." One of my daughters informed me that I obviously did not know the real words to the song. Surprised, I asked her to please enlighten me. "Mom," she emphatically replied, "The words are, 'dancing in the *sheets*.'" I couldn't believe it at first, but she was right.

The norm today is that people are allowed to do what they want to do. As Christians, we can't avoid being continually exposed to these new trends. They're all around us. There is no way to avoid suggestions of illicit sex.

Renewing the mind

To begin renewing your mind, you need to know your weakest spots. Where are you most tempted? Because you will inevitably be exposed to suggestive material, you need to know what causes you to think in ways you shouldn't.

When I was married, I could watch a wide range of movies and not think much at all about them. That's not true now. I don't go to movies just because they have a lower rating, because many of them have sex scenes. I try to stick to adventure or comedy, but no romance. If I watch something romantic—not even lustful, just romantic—I know it will be harder to keep my thoughts pure than if I don't watch it at all.

We all fantasize, some more than others. We all daydream. Instead of trying to suppress this, try to keep your daydreams godly. Suppress the temptation to fantasize about having an affair. Don't fantasize about being married to a man who is already married.

A better description of proper fantasizing is positive dreaming. There is nothing wrong with mentally picturing yourself in a situation that you would like to see happen. But instead of imagining someone you shouldn't think about, imagine yourself in a godly situation.

When you do positive dreaming, be sure that you don't start to live the dream and miss reality. That is one way affairs begin. One person starts fantasizing about being with another, which leads to the action itself, just to see if the fantasy can come true. We live much of our lives in our minds. As a James Bond theme once said, "You only live twice, or so it seems . . . one time in your life and once in your dreams."

Make sure your dreams are godly. If you are married, put your spouse in your dreams. If you can't do that, don't dream about someone else. A person just might come along or become available, and then you may be in trouble.

Believers also need models.

As Christians we are to be salt and light. We are to live in the world, but not be of the world. This is difficult, for our world has become so base that infidelity and fornication look pretty mild when compared to homosexuality, incest, and other sexual perversions. Therefore, to live as salt and light in a hardened and dark world, we can't take our models from the world. In many cases, we can't even find believers as examples. So *we* have to be salt and light to believers, as well as to unbelievers.

Your mind is *your* business. No one else really knows your thoughts but you and God. If *you* don't make the necessary changes to think properly with His help, no one will. In today's society, the battle for the mind rages fiercely every day. Our entire generation seems to be geared toward the stimulation of sexual lust. There is little hope of avoiding this stimulation totally. It's there when we drive down the street, buy groceries, go to work, go to the beach, and even in church.

We must become experts in self-knowledge. This is where the gut-level honesty begins. After looking squarely into your mind, become your own filter. Once you have discovered your area of weakness—and you know what it is—avoid it at all costs.

If a certain person arouses feelings in you that are ungodly—and he's married or unavailable, or maybe you are married—don't feed those thoughts by manipulating ways to be around him. If it is someone you can't help being around, such as a coworker, don't feed your weakness by becoming intimate friends with him.

If you can't control your thoughts about someone, put physical distance between yourself and that person. A drastic step would be a job change. But if you can't control your thoughts, you may have to face far more serious consequences than changing jobs.

What happens in the mind is the first part of the process that can lead to immorality. We often feel that "just thinking" is fairly harmless. It isn't harmless. It can lead to damaging action. It is in the thinking stage where we can most easily make positive changes, yet during that stage we are most likely to resist doing it. We still feel "safe" if we are only considering doing something. But if we continue to have improper thoughts, it is only a matter of time before we will take action. Even the next action may start with something that doesn't appear sinful, but the next and the next actions could lead to entanglements that will be difficult to reverse.

It could lead to the next step in the process toward immorality: emotional involvement.

Married Christian man after involvement with single woman at work: "In the office there is a lot of contact between the men and women. For the most part it is professional, but, as in any other situation, one encounters a lot of daily frustrations, and you deal with the problems at work, but personal problems also come into play. There's a particular point where you start talking to people, which begins as a harmless friendship. Then you cross over another line and become more dependent upon one another. You start talking about personal things in your life, and that dependency, unless it's checked and kept in its proper perspective, will continue to grow. Pretty soon, the result is an emotional attachment. That attachment can become preoccupying and lead people to do strange things."

Married Christian man after emotional involvement with single woman at work: "There's a tendency with an emotional attachment to start rationalizing your behavior. You rationalize and deny that anything is wrong. You think that you are in total control of your actions. In reality you are totally out of control."
"Emotional adultery is as damaging as physical adultery. . . . People aren't expecting to get involved emotionally. It starts out in a very subtle way. An affair isn't likely to start just out of physical lust. I think emotional attachment is a very frequent occurrence—and a very dangerous one."

Christian pastor whose relationship with married woman went from professional to emotional: "Here was a woman who had needs, and I had a need to meet her needs. So, she began to share with me difficulties she was having in her own marriage. I felt very compassionate. I saw a number of qualities in her that I began to admire. Over a period of time, I began to think her husband was a jerk because he wasn't appreciating those things. She was an intellectual stimulation to me in return. So our relationship developed over a period of time from pastor to friend, and finally we both knew it was more than that.
You know, there are all these coy little games that one can play by sending all these nonverbal messages. We got more and more involved in doing that sort of thing. Nothing was overt enough to be noticed by anyone else."

Professional Christian woman: "I became very attached to my boss. He was married and a committed Christian. We never had an affair, but my own emotional attachment to him caused me a lot of pain. I thought about him all the time, hated weekends when I was alone and he was with his family, and finally realized that I was living in a painful cross between fantasy and reality. Circumstances caused me to leave that job for another. It still took a long time to break the emotional dependency I had."

ELEVEN

"But There Was No Sexual Involvement"

Step 2: Emotional, nonphysical involvement

Complete emotional involvement

Natalie had been out of the work force for ten years. She had been working at another kind of job: that of dutiful wife and mother. But suddenly, she was faced with a situation she never imagined would happen. Her husband left her for another woman.

Natalie and her husband were both Christians. They had been very active in the local church. However, because their marriage had lacked good communication, they had tried counseling. It didn't help much, and finally, things fell apart and her husband left. The final blow was when he said he loved someone else.

Natalie began putting her life back together. She had to take care of her son, and she wanted to get on with her own commitment to the Lord in spite of what had happened. One of the counselors she and her husband had consulted asked her to be his office receptionist. Matt was the head of a small Christian counseling association. He was married, had two children, and was an ordained minister. Natalie knew the other women in the office and looked forward to the job.

Being receptionist allowed her to be in the center of all the activity of the office. She loved the work and the people. All of the counselors were married, and she had known their wives for a long time. Since Natalie hadn't started dating since her divorce, she began to throw herself fully into her work. She would stay late whenever her son had athletic practice after school and would volunteer for extra projects just to stay busy.

Matt was a wonderful boss. He encouraged her to keep busy. He praised her work, relieving her fears about being back in the work force after so many years. She respected and admired him.

Matt and Natalie occasionally had lunch together, spending long hours discussing the counseling practice and how to expand it to help more people. One day, after a particularly long lunch, one of Natalie's girlfriends asked a surprising question: "Is anything going on between you and Matt?"

"What!" was Natalie's shocked response.

"Well, you spend lots of time with him, and I just wondered if something was developing that shouldn't."

"Of course not! I like him as a friend, but that's it. There is absolutely nothing going on!"

Natalie continued the long conversations with Matt, not only about work, but about a wide range of subjects. She remained "uninvolved" with him.

Matt had become her best friend. She called him with every decision she had to make and cried with him over every frustration. She was grateful God had given her such a wonderful confidant. Matt, too, began to share his deepest feelings with her. She enjoyed having the friendship go both ways. She felt needed and secure in Matt's attention toward her.

Because nothing "sexual" was happening, Natalie continued her relationship with him. She denied that anything was wrong with seeing him and could honestly say that they were not having an "affair."

Then Matt was in an automobile accident. Natalie took the call from the emergency room notifying his office of the accident. He was not badly injured, but would be in the hospital a few days. She dashed out of the office, leaving her responsibilities to a startled secretary. As she rushed into his hospital room, she came to a screeching halt. Matt's wife was by his side. They both looked up somewhat surprised at her emotional entrance. Natalie felt her face redden, and was aware of an anger building inside of her.

"Is something wrong at the office?" Matt asked.

"No," Natalie stammered as she struggled to regain her composure. "I just wanted to see if there was anything you needed or wanted me to do."

"Natalie, that is sweet of you, but I'll take care of whatever Matt needs while he's here," his wife said.

The words cut like a hot knife. After a short chat, Natalie left, feeling hurt and cheated. She sat in her car and fought the tears of anger and humiliation. Instead of returning to work, she went home and collapsed. For the first time she honestly analyzed her relationship with Matt.

True, there had been no affair, but she had been *completely involved emotionally with someone else's husband.* She had grown to have needs for love and acceptance met by a man who could never be more than a friend.

The painful scene in the hospital room had shown her that while Matt had become *the center* of her life, she was only *a part* of his. The part Natalie thought she had been playing was being filled by his wife of many years. Natalie had no place next to his hospital bed, no place in meeting his deeper needs, no place beyond being a friend and sister in the Lord.

She had centered much of her behavior around pleasing Matt. He didn't know, of course, that she bought clothes in colors he liked, wore her hair in ways he complimented, brought desserts to the office that were his favorites. She had done it all with the justification that her behavior was okay because there was no sexual relationship.

"Sexual" doesn't have to be "physical."

The Larimers and Duncans had been friends for years. They met in Sunday school. Both men, George and Allan, were golfers, whose friendships developed over many a Saturday morning game. The women, Carol and Ann, spent hours discussing their children, church, and how to survive being golf widows.

Then George changed jobs that did not involve a move, but meant that he would be out of town much of the time. He was grateful that Carol had Allan and Ann to rely on in his absence. Allan was wonderful about coming over to fix clogged garbage disposals and broken vacuum cleaners. Carol had employed a pool service because George was gone so much, but Allan insisted that she cancel it, and so he took charge of cleaning the pool every Thursday afternoon.

If George had to be gone over a weekend, Carol would join Allan and Ann for a movie or concert. Everything seemed to be going well, and friend was helping friend.

One afternoon, Carol had an upsetting argument with her teenage son. Sobbing, she went into the bedroom and closed the door. She automatically phoned Allan. He came right over and soothed her ruffled feathers. But as other incidents upset Carol, she continued to call Allan for support. Ann never voiced any objection, nor did George.

George was gone more and more, and Carol seemed to talk less frequently to Ann. Carol assured herself that everything was proper because there was nothing sexual going on between her and Allan. But one day Allan admitted that Ann was disturbed about the amount of time he was spending with Carol. He told Carol he was sorry, but he would have to stop coming around so often. He also withdrew when she called him for emotional support.

Carol felt devastated. She took a hard look at her own marriage and had to admit that it had been sadly neglected. She had slipped into a situation where too many of her needs were being met by Allan. Again, as with Natalie, there had been no "affair," so everything appeared okay. But the truth is that *a line had been crossed.* The relationship subtly, gradually changed from just plain, good "friendship" to something inappropriate, and neither party was willing to admit it because there was nothing "sexual."

Intensity without touching

As Christians, we have often confused the words "sexual" and "physical." We say that nothing *sexual* is going on in a relationship when we really mean that nothing *physical* is going on. We are sexual beings and something "involving the sexes" is going on all the time when we relate to the opposite sex, even when no physical contact is made.

The Bible says that God "made a woman from the rib he had taken out of the man, and he brought her to the man" (Genesis 2:22). God created men and women to be companions, but He meant for them to function differently. Though the unisex philosophy of today denies it, normal men do relate as *men* and normal women do relate as *women.* So "sex" is involved. This obviously does not mean that they are relating in an act of sexual intercourse. When we say nothing "sexual" is going on, we really are implying that a couple is not engaged in sexual intercourse or the sexual activities that lead up to it.

We would be naive not to think that a great deal of "sexual" activity goes on between male and female believers. When I talk to the husband of a friend of mine, there is something sexual going on simply because he is a man and I am a woman. There is not, however, anything physical going on—and it isn't immoral. But there can be dangers in the sexual area long before the physical is ever reached. To assume that all is well because a man and woman are not touching each other physically can be overly simplistic.

A man and woman can touch each other in very meaningful ways without ever being physically close. In fact, sometimes the absence of touching can intensify feelings of attraction. Often, something that we cannot have or touch is all the more tantalizing.

Consider the relationship between Ruth and Boaz in the book of Ruth. Their encounter ends in a godly marriage, but there was a profound intensity of feeling between them that was experienced without a single touch.

We certainly don't want to become less masculine or less feminine in the way we relate to others. We do, however, want to be aware that our behavior doesn't give off the wrong signals, which could lead the other person to think something he shouldn't.

This kind of behavior falls into a gray area that can be very confusing. A long list of prohibitions is an inadequate answer. To say, for example, "One should never be alone with a married man," is unrealistic. I'm a single woman who manages a home, finances, children, and work. For me to never have a private conversation with a married man is impossible. How can I discuss private money matters if I can never be in a room with a door closed with my married financial consultant? How can a homemaker run her home and never be in contact with people who help in the maintenance and repair of that home? What if your work requires you to spend legitimate time with married male colleagues? If you have to travel, you can't avoid meeting married men also away from home. No, there's more to it than a list of what *not* to do.

It isn't the behavior that makes it ungodly. What is ungodly are the motives for the behavior, what needs you are trying to meet by that behavior, what the behavior is doing to other parties, and where it all can lead if feelings go unchecked.

Sometimes it is okay for me to have lunch with a married man and sometimes it isn't. I have to be honest with myself as to my feelings, thoughts, and desires about that person. I also need to consider what his feelings might be toward me. I have to behave differently in different situations. This is not to say that I condone situational ethics. We aren't talking about committing an immoral act just because the situation warrants it. No situation ever warrants committing an immoral act. We are talking about deciding whether even a neutral act is proper in certain situations.

When people in the world fall into immorality, there may be very little time spent in the gray area of behavior before the physical contact begins. The leap from mental to physical is usually just a tiny step.

With believers, however, *the gray area is where much game-playing occurs.* Because we tend to say that nothing is going on when there is no physical contact, we may feel safe because we think we are still walking the road of obedience—when we are really not walking obediently at all.

If we play around with our motives, tease a little, meet needs or have needs met with unavailable people, pretty soon we will fall all the way off the road of obedience into total immoral involvement and disobedience. This innocent "playing around" can lead to the next step in the process: physical contact.

TWELVE

An Innocent Little Kiss Turns Deadly

Step 3: Physical involvement—the "affair" begins

The kiss by the lake

A meeting of the Women of the Church had just ended. Dawn gathered up her papers and headed for the parking lot.

"Hi, Dawn. Got a minute?"

It was Dan, the Minister of Education.

"Sure."

He joined her at her car. He was tall and well-built—looking more like an ex-football player than a minister. Dan, his wife, and his three children had come to the church two years ago. He had been a welcome addition to the understaffed roster.

"I was wondering if you could come to my office some time this week so we could discuss how to get some of the new Women of the Church involved in teaching Sunday school."

She agreed, and they set the time.

Dawn headed home with thoughts of what to prepare for dinner. There was the usual rush to be able to make it to their son's basketball game. Pete was a junior in high school and lived for basketball. His youngest sister, Jody, was a cheerleader. "We're the 'all-American family,'" her husband, John, would often say as they watched their two offspring on the gym floor.

John was a successful attorney who was active in church and in the community. "We really *are* an all-American family," Dawn thought with pride that night as she cheered Pete's game-winning shot.

The next day's meeting with Dan was routine. This became the first of many such meetings over the winter months. There was much to do. She enjoyed talking with Dan. He was a good conversationalist. He seemed to have time to listen and had interesting things to share when he wasn't listening. Often, they would get into deep discussions on religion and theology.

When Dawn would tell John about some of these talks, he would shake his head, amused that two people could enjoy such abstract philosophical matters. He, on the other hand, loved to talk about law and strategy, court cases and trials—things with definite procedures and precedents. Dawn would listen to his stories with the same disinterest as he did to hers. But that was okay. They didn't have much time for serious conversation between his work, her volunteer work, and the kids' activities.

Spring came and life rolled on as usual. One afternoon when Dawn and Dan had ended one of their long conversations, he suggested they go for a walk around a nearby lake instead of staying cooped up in the office. They drove out of town with the car windows down and the radio playing. Dawn felt good. She felt young and free. It was good to have a little change of scenery—nothing wrong with that.

Since it was a weekday, the lake was deserted. They began to walk around on the well-worn path, evidence that this was generally a very populated spot. The conversation shifted somewhere along the way from theology to spring and spring fever and young love and love and. . . .

They were standing perfectly still, facing one another. Dawn felt like a school girl . . . and yet, she knew . . . but *she ignored the small voice inside her, warning her to leave.*

That brief encounter was the beginning. It was a simple kiss. A mistake. Yes, a human mistake. It was a combination of the weather and being with a good friend. Dawn ran all these rationalizations through her mind again and again. She and Dan did not even discuss what had happened. They had laughed, embarrassed for the moment at their actions, and dismissed it. Their friendship went on as before. In fact, it seemed even better. Instead of feeling uncomfortable about what had happened, Dan and Dawn seemed to enjoy a new level of communication.

But Dawn kept picturing that moment by the lake. It had been exciting. She wondered if it would ever happen again. Of *course* it wouldn't! Dan was a dedicated pastor, committed to the Lord and to his family. She was a committed Christian, too.

But it did happen again. And again. And, soon, more happened. By summer, Dan and Dawn were making excuses to keep meeting even when church activities slowed down. They succeeded in keeping up a front, and continued to meet at least weekly during the summer.

Of course, they tried to see each other legitimately for church business and stop the affair, but those efforts kept weakening. They would pray together and vow not to slip again. But they did slip. It was a full-fledged affair.

It became necessary to tell little white lies. There was also the growing problem of how to relate to their spouses in the proper way when they felt so deeply for one another. They kept telling themselves that they were hurting no one else and that soon they would have the will power to end the affair and just be good friends again.

But it didn't end.

So many lies, so much deceit, so much sin. What could they do? How had it happened? Who else would be hurt?

The web of intrigue widens, affecting others.

We do not live on islands. Adultery never hurts only the two people involved. The web of intrigue and deceit becomes so consuming that all other areas of life suffer in the attempt to live out a charade.

The classic biblical example of adultery is the account of David and Bathsheba. David—a man after God's own heart. Bathsheba—the wife of Uriah. Uriah—a faithful soldier in David's army.

David apparently slept with Bathsheba only one time. The Bible says, "He slept with her. . . .Then she went back home" (2 Samuel 11:4). We aren't told, but David may have even determined not to see her again. But she got pregnant. The sin that David may have thought he had gotten away with now needed covering up. He planned to get Uriah home and in bed with Bathsheba so it would appear that the pregnancy was from him and that David's sin would go undetected.

But Uriah, a good soldier, wanted to be with his men. He said, "The ark and Israel and Judah are staying in tents, and my master Joab and my lord's men are camped in the open fields. How could I go to my house to eat and drink and lie with my wife? As surely as you live, I will not do such a thing!" (2 Samuel 11:11).

David *had* to cover up this sin. He was a man of God, and could not let his testimony be ruined. So he sent out the order. "Put Uriah in the front line where the fighting is fiercest. Then withdraw from him so he will be struck down and die" (2 Samuel 11:15).

How many Uriahs suffer from the sins of another? Satan may whisper that no one else is being hurt. But that is a lie. Other sins come in to cover the first one. The most obvious is lying. Coveting was there from the beginning. One deceitful act follows another.

Though the Christian community says loudly and clearly that it considers adultery wrong, many Christians aren't living that way. We are becoming like Ahab: "Ahab son of Omri did more evil in the eyes of the LORD than any of those before him. He not only considered it trivial to commit the sins of Jeroboam . . . but he also married Jezebel . . . and began to serve Baal and worship him" (1 Kings 16:30-31).

Considered it *trivial*? Do we really consider it trivial to commit adultery? The standard phrase among many believers caught in adultery is that God will forgive them—and they go on, get a divorce, and marry the adulterous partner. Active in the church again, life goes on as if the adultery and divorce were mistakes in the past that are now forgiven and forgotten.

It is true that "if we confess our sins, [God] is faithful and just and will forgive us our sins and purify us from all unrighteousness" (1 John 1:9). It seems, however, that confession and repentance doesn't occur until after a divorce and remarriage with the new partner. What about the sins against the offended partner? What about Uriah? Most Christians don't kill their mates. They just walk away from them and start over.

Once you cross the threshold of involvement with a married person, the chances of turning around and not hurting anyone else are minimal. The power of this sin is so strong that breaking off the relationship becomes a herculean task.

Dawn and Dan tried to stop seeing each other. They tried to get their relationship back to a friendship. They called out their spiritual reserves and prayed, read the Bible, and memorized Scripture. But when the flesh and Satan are on the same side, the Lord can't change us without our help. We have to be willing to suffer frustration of the flesh to operate under the control of the Holy Spirit.

The mistake that Dawn and Dan kept making was that they kept on seeing each other. They enjoyed the gratification and wanted to hang on to it at all costs. If they could just get it back to friendship, they could still be together and not be committing a sin. But that was just falling prey to rationalization, the final step that *keeps* people in an immoral relationship.

THIRTEEN

"I'm Only Human"

Step 4: Rationalizations for continuing the affair

Human nature isn't an excuse.

Cynthia and Tom met at the singles class at their church. Both had been divorced several years before, and now felt ready to begin dating again. Cynthia accepted Christ during the recovery stages of her divorce. Tom was a professing Christian for only a short time.

Cynthia, who married in her early twenties, was now in her late thirties. She had thought life would be easier: Meet your future husband at college, fall in love, marry after graduation, have two children, and live happily ever after. She did all that—except living happily ever after. By this time in her life, she should have been leading the PTA and hostessing parties for her husband's office staff. Instead, she was back in the work force and raising her children alone.

She had always attended church. It was the socially acceptable thing to do. But when divorce shattered her well-ordered world, the shallow go-to-church-on-Sunday brand of religion offered little real comfort. One of her friends introduced her to the meaning of a personal relationship with Jesus Christ, as opposed to superficial religiosity. Though the pain of her divorce wasn't removed, she had a new meaning in life and loving help through the trauma.

Cynthia hadn't even thought about dating the first year after the divorce, but the loneliness was a very real and awful experience. She had joined the office girls for the "bar scene," but found it uncomfortable and contrary to her growing relationship with Christ. Wanting to date only believers, she decided to join the singles class at church.

Tom had waited till his thirties to get married. The marriage lasted only a few years and produced no children. He started dating again, but also felt lonely and empty. Some of his office buddies had started attending church as a result of the singles ministry. He joined them one Sunday and realized, after hearing the gospel, that he had been seeking fulfillment in the wrong places. A relationship with Jesus Christ made sense to him, and so he prayed for Christ to come in and change his life.

He met Cynthia in the singles group. They began dating. Gradually, they began to spend more time together, with Tom joining Cynthia and her children at her home for dinner. It was a comfortable, unpressured situation. They both enjoyed the relaxed, family-style time together. It reminded them of some of the better days of their previous marriages.

The physical involvement began innocently enough with a good night kiss at the door one evening when Tom left for home. Both of them had no intentions of compromising their biblical standards in the moral realm and had agreed at the beginning that they would keep their relationship pure.

But they soon began having sexual intercourse on a regular basis. It was never planned, always marred by guilt, never gave the emotional fulfillment they longed for, and they always determined to never let it happen again. However, it did and did and did. "After all," they thought, "we're only human."

Many single Christians rationalize their affairs.

In the single-adult Christian community, unfortunately, this scenario is quite common. Singles should be aware of this before they enter or reenter the dating scene. It isn't biblical, but it is how things are.

Paul addressed this issue in 1 Corinthians 7:8-9: "Now to the unmarried and the widows I say: It is good for them to stay unmarried, as I am. But if they cannot control themselves, they should marry, for it is better to marry than to burn with passion."

Many Christians singles are doing neither—marrying or burning. Instead of marrying, there is an attitude among many to "put off" that binding commitment. And instead of burning, they take part in illicit sex because they are "only human."

Some Christian men have admitted to me that they are afraid to get married or to remarry. They can avoid the involvement and still get all the sex they need. In their view, they have the best of both worlds. In fact, one Christian single said, in reference to this passage in Corinthians, "*That* is not a good reason to get married."

I agree that to marry someone just because you want to have sex is poor judgment and *not* a good reason to marry. If, however, you are unable to live a life of chastity as a single believer, being married *is* certainly a better state in which to "work out your salvation" (Philippians 2:12).

We also have a "spiritual" nature.

Today's culture has so watered down the chastity issue that even the Christian community has settled for a watered-down solution on how to live with unfulfilled desires. We aren't "only" human. If we belong to Christ, we are also "spirit." Naturally, the fallen human side of us doesn't disappear when we come to Christ, but there is now present within us "a spirit of power, of love and of self-discipline" (2 Timothy 1:7). We have help to live a godly life—not perfectly, but in a determined, thoughtful, and disciplined way. Therefore, to say "I'm only human" and then give in to ungodly desires is a gross rationalization.

Can a thief say, "I'm only human," after stealing something and expect to go unpunished, then repeat the crime again and again? Can a businessman cheat because of an "only human" desire to succeed and then expect to go unpunished if discovered? Yet, in matters of immorality, there seems to be a sense that one should be forgiven, go unpunished, and then accepted by the Christian community. There seems to be no sense of responsibility for one's actions. How has this whole rationalizing process crept into Christian ethics?

Rationalizations for continuing an affair

Affairs between believers go on and on because of a lack of total honesty. It's called rationalization. Some excuses given are:

"Just one more time."

"If my husband (or wife) only met my needs, I wouldn't do this."

"I understand him (her) so much better than his wife (her husband) does."

"He (she) needs me."

"We minister together."

"It won't happen again."

"I'm just too weak."

"If only God would give me the strength to stop."

"God knows that I need this."

"So many others are doing it; it can't be that bad."

"No one else knows, so what's the harm?"

"God will forgive us."

"There are worse sins."

"God loves us no matter what we do."

Some of these statements, such as the last one, are true. But that's not the whole story. It is really very simple. The Bible says, "You shall not commit adultery" (Exodus 20:14). There is no way to rationalize it. God is serious about this offense.

Why are so many Christians caught up in immorality? I think it is because they haven't looked honestly at themselves early enough. *It's back to the process.* If earlier on they would have been aware that they were getting caught in a web of sin, they might have been able to disentangle themselves before getting totally entangled. Once a physical involvement begins, control becomes very difficult.

Once over the line in total sexual involvement, a decision has to be made. If you belong to the Lord, you cannot go on indefinitely in an immoral relationship and expect anything other than grief. You have to make a decision. And it must be made *today.*

PART IV

The Pathway Back to Godliness

FOURTEEN

The Day of Decision

Step 1: Reestablishing a relationship with Christ

If you are now in the middle of an affair or in the process that could lead to one, you can't muddle on any longer. Perhaps you have decided numerous times to stop, but you haven't been able to give it up.

Not this time! This time a final decision must be made. No more fence-sitting. And, ironically, the decision is not to lead a godly life. The decision is not to change how you are. It isn't a decision that will result in a neat, problem-free life.

The decision you need to make now is one you may have made once before, but the vitality of it has died. It is the kind of decision that, if you have *not* made it before, you need to make now. You must either accept or reject it. It is the *only* decision that can give you the power to live the life you desire and that God desires for you.

Before explaining this crucial decision, let's summarize:

The problem—One of the growing problems that challenges the Christian community today is that of sexual immorality. It is damaging relationships between individuals, and between individuals and the Lord. The results are broken homes and broken lives. The Christian community is not immune to the devastation of sexual immorality. It can be, and *is*, infected by this sinful venom.

The awareness of a process—There is a process that leads a person from one step to another on the road to immorality. Awareness of this process is the first step in dealing with the problem. *All* of us are susceptible to becoming entangled in this process.

Now, what to do?

The decision

How many times have you "decided" to keep a New Year's resolution? How many times have you decided to go on a diet? How many times have you decided to save a certain amount of money each month? How many times have you decided to exercise regularly, get organized, read, study, or pray? And how many times have you really succeeded in maintaining your decision? Most of us just decide to change, but then never act on that decision.

Being a committed Christian does not mean that once we accept Christ, we will then begin immediately to live a godly life. We simply don't have the power to do that any more than we have the power to keep all those other resolutions we make.

What we do have is the opportunity to enter into a new or renewed *relationship* with Jesus Christ. After entering into that relationship, it is with His power, and that of the Holy Spirit, that we are enabled to live godly lives.

You are probably saying, "I've already *done* that. I've accepted Christ and I still don't have any power." If you have truly accepted Him, the key question is: Have you let "rules and regulations" or the "relationship" with Christ guide your life?

If you accept Christ and then try to live a list of "dos and don'ts," you will fail. If, however, you live to know Him and cultivate a relationship with Him, then *living a godly life will be the normal byproduct of that relationship.* The way out of immorality is a process, too.

In relating to people we care about, we are able to do the best for them because of our love for them. We are able to be self-sacrificing and giving because the relationship is more important than our own desires. If our relationship with Jesus Christ becomes also more important than our own desires, we will live more godly lives because we will try to please Him.

If we try to "live the list" simply because we are "supposed" to, but fail to develop a relationship with the Lord, then we will undoubtedly fail. This is precisely why a number of Christians have fallen into immorality: They are trying to live a list. And a list has no power. You don't have devotions in order to end an immoral relationship; you have devotions in order to establish a strong relationship with Christ. Then the power and the love in the relationship with Him enables you to end the sexual affair.

What is the distinction between living a list based on our own determination and living a godly life as a result of a relationship with Jesus Christ? What is the decision to be made? In order to better understand this, let's investigate how Jesus and His disciples related.

The invitation

Matthew 4:18-20 describes the first calling of the disciples: "As Jesus was walking beside the Sea of Galilee, he saw two brothers, Simon called Peter and his brother Andrew. They were casting a net into the lake, for they were fishermen. 'Come, follow me,' Jesus said, 'and I will make you fishers of men.' At once they left their nets and followed him."

Jesus must have presented to them a life better than the one they were leading for them to drop their nets and immediately follow Him. Jesus offers us a better life, too. In fact, eternal life. He invites us to follow Him—to change direction and walk with Him.

We must decide to follow Him and enter into a meaningful relationship with Him, or to return to what we were doing when He first became known to us.

Walking with Him

"Jesus went throughout Galilee, teaching in their synagogues, preaching the good news of the kingdom, and healing every disease and sickness among the people. . . . When he saw the crowds, he went up on a mountainside and sat down. His disciples came to him, and he began to teach them . . ." (Matthew 4:23, 5:1-2).

Early in their relationship with the Lord, the disciples were *with* Him and *listened* to His teaching. Today, as we establish a relationship with the Lord, we can also walk with Him and listen to His teaching. We do this by reading the Bible, praying, learning from more mature Christians, and fellowshiping with other believers.

The early disciples walked with Jesus because of Jesus. They saw Him face-to-face and were given the ability to believe that He was who He said He was.

We do not see Jesus Christ face-to-face, but we do have the Holy Spirit to reveal Him to us. Jesus said, "When he, the Spirit of truth, comes, he will guide you into all truth" (John 16:13). The power to live godly lives comes with the genuine commitment to enter into a relationship with the Lord.

What Jesus taught

In Matthew 5-7 (the Sermon on the Mount), Jesus Christ taught many of the core principles necessary for living the Christian life. The disciples had already entered into a relationship with Him by the time He delivered that sermon. Living out what He taught was based on their established relationship with Him, not on their ability to live what He taught.

The disciples undoubtedly wanted to obey what their Master taught because of Him, not just because of the teachings, for the Pharisees had been teaching the law for centuries. The result of their teaching was dry legalism.

At the end of the Sermon on the Mount, Jesus issued a warning to those who would not follow His teachings:

> "Therefore everyone who hears these words of mine and puts them into practice is like a wise man who built his house on the rock. The rain came down, the streams rose, and the winds blew and beat against that house; yet it did not fall, because it had its foundation on the rock. But everyone who hears those words of mine and does not put them into practice is like a foolish man who built his house on sand. The rain came down, the streams rose, and the winds blew and beat against that house, and it fell with a great crash."
>
> When Jesus had finished saying these things, the crowds were amazed at his teaching, because he taught as one who had authority, and not as their teachers of the law. (Matthew 7:24-29)

The relationship the disciples had with Jesus was not threatened by His teachings. He taught about the blessings of obeying Him, as well as the consequences of not obeying. But the relationship, because it was real, was still there.

Jesus also made it clear that apart from a relationship with Him, there is no access to God. The keeping of the law alone would account for nothing. That takes care of the "lists"!

Elements of a genuine relationship with Christ

"Not everyone who says to me, 'Lord, Lord,' will enter the kingdom of heaven, but only he who does the will of my Father who is in heaven. Many will say to me on that day, 'Lord, Lord, did we not prophesy in your name, and in your name drive out demons and perform many miracles?' Then I will tell them plainly, 'I never knew you. Away from me, you evildoers!'" (Matthew 7:21-23).

If not all the people who say they are Christians really are, then how can we know who is for real? What are the elements of a genuine relationship with Jesus Christ? Here are five spiritual indications of a life committed to Christ:

1. Believing

The disciples believed. In Matthew 8:23-26, we see the disciples with Jesus in a boat. When a storm comes up, the disciples are afraid. They awaken Jesus. "He replied, 'You of little faith, why are you so afraid?' Then he got up and rebuked the winds and the waves, and it was completely calm."

The friends of the paralytic man believed. "Jesus stepped into a boat, crossed over and came to his own town. Some men brought to him a paralytic, lying on a mat. When Jesus saw their faith, he said to the paralytic, 'Take heart, son; your sins are forgiven'" (Matthew 9:1-2).

The woman believed. "Just then a woman who had been subject to bleeding for twelve years came up behind him and touched the edge of his cloak. She said to herself, 'If I only touch his cloak, I will be healed.' Jesus turned and saw her. 'Take heart, daughter,' he said, 'your faith has healed you.' And the woman was healed from that moment" (Matthew 9:20-22).

Committed, active faith is the beginning of a genuine relationship with Christ. It is a faith that believes that Jesus is who He says He is, and that what He says is true.

In our relationships with others, it is essential that we can be able to believe what they say. If not, the relationships will deteriorate. If we say we have a relationship with Christ, but do not believe, or if we behave in a manner that shows we don't truly believe, then we need to reevaluate the genuineness of our relationship. Jesus is faithful. If there is doubt, it is our fault.

2. Loving

"'These people honor me with their lips, but their hearts are far from me. They worship me in vain; their teachings are but rules taught by men'" (Matthew 15:8-9).

"Hearing that Jesus had silenced the Sadducees, the Pharisees got together. One of them, an expert in the law, tested him with this question: 'Teacher, which is the greatest commandment in the Law?' Jesus replied: '"Love the Lord your God with all your heart and with all your soul and with all your mind." This is the first and greatest commandment'" (Matthew 22:34-38).

A person with a heart that loves God does not see a list of strict rules to follow. He or she sees a relationship with a perfectly faithful and loving friend. Instead of restriction, there is freedom. Instead of pain, there is comfort. Instead of things to do, there is a person for whom to do them.

Loving Jesus Christ will produce a life of willing obedience. Though obedience will never be perfect in this life, the love behind it will motivate a believer toward godliness.

3. Acknowledging

"'But what about you?' he asked. 'Who do you say I am?' Simon Peter answered, 'You are the Christ, the Son of the living God'" (Matthew 16:15-16).

It is important to realize that the object of our faith and love is actually God Himself. Jesus, in His relationship with His disciples, made it clear to them that He was God the Son. When Peter said, "You are the Christ," Jesus responded by saying, "Blessed are you. . . ." In our relationship with Christ, we have no grounds to believe that He could begin to do what He claims He can do if He is not God.

4. Understanding

"From that time on Jesus began to explain to his disciples that he must go to Jerusalem and suffer many things at the hands of the elders, chief priests and teachers of the law, and that he must be killed and on the third day be raised to life" (Matthew 16:21).

Understanding the mission of Jesus allows us to understand why we can be free. If we do not understand what Jesus did for us, we will not be able to have a lasting commitment to Him.

Because of who He is and what He did, our personal relationship with Him is not like any other we experience. It is not a temporary friendship with a wonderful person. It is a permanent commitment with the living God, resulting in eternal life.

5. Obeying

"Watch out for false prophets. They come to you in sheep's clothing, but inwardly they are ferocious wolves. By their fruit you will recognize them. Do people pick grapes from thornbushes, or figs from thistles? Likewise every good tree bears good fruit, but a bad tree bears bad fruit. A good tree cannot bear bad fruit, and a bad tree cannot bear good fruit. Every tree that does not bear good fruit is cut down and thrown into the fire. Thus, by their fruit you will recognize them" (Matthew 7:15-20).

"We know that anyone born of God does not continue to sin; the one who was born of God keeps him safe, and the evil one cannot harm him. We know that we are children of God, and that the whole world is under the control of the evil one. We know also that the Son of God has come and has given us understanding, so that we may know him who is true. And we are in him who is true—even in his Son Jesus Christ. He is the true God and eternal life" (1 John 5:18-20).

Obedience is the fruit of a genuine relationship with Jesus Christ. The obedience we attempt is less than perfect. So what do we do when confronted with a particular sin?

The account of Peter is a classic example of a true believer caught in the sin of denying Christ. When Peter realized what he had done he "went outside and wept bitterly" (Matthew 26:75).

If we have a true relationship with Jesus Christ and we become aware of a sin in our lives, we will weep bitterly. The work of repentance will cause the true believer to want to change. If there is no feeling of sorrow over hurting our Lord, we need to really evaluate if Jesus is really our Lord at all.

We see that Peter was restored to fellowship with the Lord. He was with the disciples when Jesus appeared to them after His resurrection. After they saw Him, they (including Peter) worshiped Him.

"If we claim to be without sin, we deceive ourselves and the truth is not in us. If we confess our sins, he is faithful and just and will forgive us our sins and purify us from all unrighteousness" (1 John

1:8-9). As we seek to walk obediently, we are motivated out of love for Christ. When we fail, we are able to ask forgiveness and begin again.

Your decision

You can begin to win the battle of immorality only by having a new or renewed relationship with Jesus Christ. This is not a decision assuring that you will never be tempted again. But it does show that you desire to put the relationship with Christ above your own desires.

Just as there is a process that leads to immorality, there is also a process that leads away from it toward a godly lifestyle. The first step of the process back to God is to make the relationship with Christ number one in importance in your life. The decision is not to stop immorality, but to follow Him.

Decide now to commit to Jesus—or decide not to. If you claim to belong to Him, decide to make that relationship a priority. If you don't want to do that, stop claiming that you belong to Him and stop further degrading His name by your behavior.

Jesus said, "He who is not with me is against me . . ." (Matthew 12:30). When you say that you are with Christ, you are not making a commitment never to sin again. You are making a commitment to make your relationship with the living God the number-one priority in your life.

The difference between this commitment to Christ and any you may have made in the past is that *this* time you are putting your relationship with Him in the forefront of your awareness. The first time your commitment may have been to gain eternal life. But with this commitment you are saying to the Lord that *He* is important to you . . . that you desire a meaningful relationship with Him . . . that living as He says to live is important to you because it is important to Him . . . that He will be the Lord of all you say, think and do . . . the Lord of your life.

If He is first, then relationships with others will only be fulfilling if they are ones He would approve of. If Christ is Lord of your life, there will be a power present to begin the process of turning from situations that are ungodly. When you decide to establish (or reestablish) a relationship with Christ, you have taken the first step in the process back to godliness.

Commitment To Follow Christ

1. SALVATION - ETERNAL LIFE
2. BLESSINGS & HEALINGS
3. PRIORITY

Christian man after close friend's marriage is threatened by adultery: "In retrospect, my wife and I saw many occasions where we could identify communication problems in our friend's marriage, but we said nothing. He became involved with another married woman and subsequently left his wife for her. My wife and I now see (1) that we should have voiced our concerns and (2) that we would now never refrain from speaking out in the future with other friends where we see similar difficulties.

"We were hesitant to speak out because we were fearful about jeopardizing the friendship. But now, we would see that risk as being far less significant than the pain both couples went through as a result of the unresolved tensions in their marriage.

"I would now never hesitate to risk a friendship for the sake of saving a marriage."

Christian man after involvement with coworker: "I have asked some Christian friends at work to hold me accountable. When you lack accountability, you are wide open for rationalization. Accountability really strengthens you. It is a reminder to keep your priorities straight."

FIFTEEN

Back to Godliness

Step 2: Ending the immoral relationship

Some who ended the affair

Helen and John—Helen and John had been having an adulterous affair on and off for about six months. They had come to realize that they simply couldn't end it. Both of them had been committed Christians who were now at the brink of ruining two families and their own testimonies.

They worked for the same Christian organization, and had sincerely tried to go back to being "just friends" and coworkers. For a time, they would succeed. Then one of them would weaken and they would succumb to their sexual desires.

Their friends had begun to notice the amount of time they spent together. There were some casual comments. In desperation, they were ready to get counseling help. They were ready to do whatever it would take to right the situation.

Nancy—Nancy recognized, with growing irritation, that her dependence on her boss was unhealthy. She had spent months justifying her feelings by telling herself everything was okay because they were not romantically involved.

She had even told him that they should spend less time together, and when they were together to talk less intimately. But he brushed aside her concerns as foolish, and temporarily convinced her that God had brought them together to be a comfort to each other. She knew that they were just kidding themselves about their friendship.

She was right. It soon went beyond inappropriate behavior into a full-fledged affair. Even if Nancy's boss was not willing to take action, she was. She began taking the necessary steps to break her dependency on him.

Marlene—Marlene was spending more and more time alone. She had dropped out of her Bible study group and had only minimal contact with her Christian friends. Much of her time was spent at work and watching TV at home.

Her fantasy world had become her refuge. She would slip into the characters on the TV screen or in the pages of the novel she was reading. Friends began to call her attention to the fact that she seemed "somewhere else" when they did get to see her. She realized that she had allowed her thought life to control her. She fantasized about things she wanted to happen in her life that weren't happening. She pictured herself romantically involved with a number of men she knew only casually.

She felt nothing was wrong with this because no one else knew of her thoughts and she had taken no action on them . . . yet. But when her boss scolded her about not paying attention to her job, she became disgusted with herself and decided to get help.

Starting the process back to godliness

Just as there is a process that leads to immorality, there is also a process that leads back to godliness. There is no instant cure.

1. *The acknowledgment of sin*—The first step in this process of restoration is an acknowledgment of sin. Rationalization must end. The situation must be seen for what it really is in God's eyes. We can no longer look at the affair with the eyes of the world or even with our own weakened "spiritual" eyes.

We can no longer compare ourselves to other believers who may be caught in more damaging sins than our own. God is looking at us individually—in light of His Son and His Word, not in light of the world around us.

We must become convicted of our sins. Jerry Bridges addressed this issue of conviction when he said, "'A belief is what you hold; a conviction is what holds you.' A conviction is not authentic unless it includes a commitment to live accordingly."

In acknowledging sin, we must do more than just believe it is wrong. We must be convicted enough to be willing to change. And that conviction must grip us personally. We will be able to find people, even in Christian circles, who will excuse sin, thus influencing us to rationalize our bad thoughts, behavior, or involvement.

Acknowledgment and conviction go hand in hand. We begin at 1 John 1:8-9: "If we claim to be without sin, we deceive ourselves and the truth is not in us. If we confess our sins, he is faithful and just and will forgive us our sins and purify us from all unrighteousness." After confessing and asking for forgiveness, we are ready for action.

2. *Take action immediately*—The process that leads back to godliness is different than the one that led away from the spiritual walk. In moving away from God, the process may be slow and subtle. In moving back to God, the action must be deliberate, quick, and radical.

By radical, I mean we must make decisions and stick to them, even if they later seem to have been too harsh. We need to take quick action because procrastination will only make it even harder to get started on the renewing process.

Being deliberate means making a commitment to follow through. We are not saying we will *try* to go back to a godly lifestyle; we need to definitely *commit* to going back to a godly lifestyle. And this commitment will work only if we have first made the personal, relational commitment to Jesus Christ, as mentioned in the previous chapter. Seeing that our relationship with Him is more important than our relationship with any other person is the only way we will win the battle.

3. *Actions must be based on obedience*—The process that led away from godliness was based primarily on feelings and emotions. We may have had rational, godly thoughts during our time of drifting away, but they were rendered ineffective because the decisions at the time were based on emotions.

Now, on the road back to godliness, actions based on obedience to Him must rule over actions based on what you *feel* you want to do. There is a saying, "You can't feel yourself into a new way of acting; you have to act yourself into a new way of feeling."

You will want to continue seeing the other person; you won't want to hurt him or her; you'll still have lustful feelings for the other person (your tendency will be to continue to ignore them). The discipline of taking immediate action is much easier said than done.

As Christians we sometimes overlook the fact that sin is fun. That is the great enticement to begin with. The power of sin is real, and it takes great strength to break it.

Getting out of immoral involvement—cold turkey

The most effective way to end an adulterous relationship is *cold turkey.* No more contact of any kind.

Once the decision has been made to end the affair, there must be a final goodbye. No more discussions about what went wrong, no more attempts to be "just friends," no more brief phone calls for just a little advice. No more contact!

You may feel there are very legitimate reasons to contact the other person. But, as a leading psychologist said to me, "If one person in an adulterous affair calls the other after the breakup—the person called must *hang up* the phone." Sound harsh? It is, but it is the only way. We are dealing with a very destructive force and it must be dealt with harshly.

I have a friend who took the advice of a competent Christian counselor, and was able to end an immoral relationship. When he told her to hang up when her boyfriend called, she did not feel she would be able to do so. She actually practiced picking up the phone, imagining him saying "hello," and then hanging up. Her friend did call; she did hang up; she did break the relationship; she did grow strong in the Lord.

Satan will be relentless in trying to get you back with your lover. Weeks will go by and you won't hear from the other person. Then, "out of the blue," you may see him. Because some time has passed, you may feel safe in resuming the relationship on a different level.

There will be a tendency to gravitate back toward the former lover instead of maintaining a distance. Remember, we are talking about abruptly ending a relationship with someone you have grown emotionally attached to, someone you feel you love. Your heart will fight against the decision made by obedience to the Word.

Time and maturity in the Lord *may* allow for some form of friendship in the future. But, in the beginning of a deliberate reversal in lifestyle, friendship shouldn't even be considered. That isn't the issue. The issue is your committed relationship with Jesus Christ. He says emphatically and repeatedly in His Word that adultery is wrong.

Because of that, you must give it up and turn the affair over to Him. Whether a friendship is possible or not will be for Him to determine.

What if the two people work together? A job change for one of them *may* be the only solution. If they are in a large enough organization where they do not have to have contact, they may be able to make it. But the battle will be fiercer and longer if the temptation is close by.

Why such drastic measures? Because it is the only way a reversal will work. The flesh is weak and Satan is clever. He will deceive you just enough to make you think that you can successfully take two steps back and not slip again. When you think you are safe, the desire to be intimate will surge to the surface, perhaps stronger than ever before. And you'll fall again.

A safeguard for maintaining distance is to confide in someone you are accountable to. In most cases of adultery, the help of a trained counselor is necessary to help resolve the situation. He or she will be a source of encouragement and direction when the decision to change becomes difficult to continue. And a counselor will keep it in the strictest confidence. A *trusted* friend may also be of great help. Do make sure that the friend is not someone who will share your situation in the form of a prayer request.

Because the backlash of an adulterous relationship can be so disastrous, before confessing to your spouse or trying to repair your life by yourself, seek professional help. If you are not familiar with whom to contact, check with your pastor for the name of a trained counselor in your area. In the meantime, make the decision to break the contact—and break it!

Don't be surprised if . . .

1. *Don't be surprised if you start off strongly and falter quickly.* Once you have decided to end an immoral relationship, you will probably feel great relief and determination. Don't be shocked or caught off guard if that determination is challenged almost instantly. Patterns are difficult to break, especially sexual ones.

Also, remember that you have an adversary. Satan doesn't want you to win this battle. He will sneak back into your thoughts in many ways. You will find yourself thinking, "What I was doing wasn't so bad after all"; "Compared to everyone else, I'm okay"; "I can't help myself"; and on and on.

And so the rationalization stage will begin again. When this starts to happen, realize that you are being led back to making decisions based on *feelings.* You were determined yesterday. Good. You feel helpless today. That's okay, too. But don't take action based on either of these feelings. It is good to *feel* determined, but the real basis for your action is founded on biblical truth and conviction to put Christ first in your life. Biblical truth doesn't change with feelings. The truth that allowed you to choose right actions yesterday is still the truth that you may be trying to rationalize about today.

Don't contact the person with whom you've broken up; don't fantasize about being with him; don't try endlessly to get out of your pain. Accept the pain as a result of disobedience, then move forward with correct behavior. Enlist all the spiritual armor you can. Determine to be faithful to the Lord.

2. *Don't be surprised if fear becomes a constant companion.* Fear, other than proper godly fear of the Lord, is debilitating. You may think fearful things you've never thought before: being rejected because of your mistakes; never again having the titillating feelings you just gave up; never feeling so deeply about someone again.

A spirit of fear does not come from the Lord. When fear comes in, recognize the presence of the enemy. Satan wants you to lose. Go back to the basics. Stay close to the Lord and refuse to allow fear to control you.

Above all, don't go back to any of the old behavioral patterns just to relieve the fears. If you fear feeling unloved, don't go to some counterfeit source to try to get love.

3. *Don't be surprised if you need to act out of sheer obedience.* This is a real battle. Your strong convictions and determination will last only if you admit to the severity of the predicament you are in. Rationalization will fight the truth. But you must fight fear with peace. You will *want* to return to old sinful patterns. You will even have thoughts of justification similar to the ones that allowed you to get involved in the first place.

The process away from godliness progressed with an element of excitement and pleasure. The process back to godliness is a painful, uphill battle all the way. You will be going against the wind. This requires strength. You will feel weak because it takes a great deal of energy to fight this battle.

You may need to drop some activities and rearrange major parts of your life. Take all the time you need. Make all the alterations necessary. You'll be able to participate in the work of the Kingdom again when you are well. Emotional illness is every bit as debilitating as physical illness.

When you feel weak, hang on in the Lord's strength. Obey out of sheer willingness to obey. You don't need to *feel* like obeying. Do it anyway. You don't need to feel strong to obey. After you have taken action to break the contact with the one you've had the affair with, your next action may be one of sitting still and resting before the Lord. However, be constantly on guard when you are still, or your mind may drift back to the times you've just left behind.

Accept help

You have been in a battle. Now you are in another one, but of a different nature. God desires you to walk with Him. Satan wants you, too.

You are weak and weary. You may still be confused. You want to stay committed to putting Christ first, but the old ways require so little energy, and the change back to godliness seems to require so much effort. That's why you need to take advantage of any godly means available to you to win the battle.

Bring a friend into your confidence for support and accountability. Begin attending a Sunday school class or Bible study. Cultivate meaningful relationships with committed, mature believers.

None of these things will prevent immorality. They may encourage you, however, to stay on the right path. They will be strong, positive influences. God does use His people in the lives of others to help change them. Be open to Him to provide support through others, and also through His Word, His Spirit, and the written words of other believers.

PART V

The World of Work

Professional Christian businessman: "They call me 'the preacher' at work. That title provides more of a challenge for me. Just this morning, I went into work and this woman in the office came over to ask me something. She leaned up against me in a provocative way. I just pulled back like I didn't notice and walked away. . . . Every morning I get up and ask for protection from scandalous sin. I get this from the Lord's Prayer: 'Lead us not into temptation.'"

Professional Christian woman: "In the past, I did not think much about being behind closed doors with a man. Now, I am careful about how often and the amount of time a door is closed. Even if nothing is inappropriate, I try to be sensitive to putting myself and someone else in a potentially compromising position."

Professional Christian businessman, speaking about his own behavior in an office setting: "It would be nice if we could step back and take a look at our own behavior and see ourselves as others see us. That might make us stop [questionable behavior] more quickly."

SIXTEEN

The Business World

The uniqueness of the office

Working in an office is a fact of life for many men and for a growing number of women, too. It is so much a part of everyday life that many of us tend to take it for granted. We get up, go to work, leave work, go home, sleep, and go to work again. It takes up one third of our twenty-four hours in a day. The primary exception to this routine is the mother who is at home raising children. We will look at her relation to the "office phenomenon" at the end of this chapter.

We go to work routinely with little thought to the uniqueness of our work place. There are volumes of books on the atmosphere, attitudes, activities, and structure of the home. There are also volumes published on the business world with regard to management, strategies, attitudes for success, and effectiveness in business.

But what about books on the unique dynamics of the office and relationships in that arena where we spend so much of our time? There are factors in our work world that greatly affect our thinking and behavior, that challenge our morals and integrity. We are aware of these as they relate to the business we are engaged in, but we need to also be aware of them with regard to the way we relate to the people around us.

Office atmosphere

Electricity. Energy. Motion. Excitement. Stress. Pressure. Weariness. Performance.

Five days a week, most of us walk into an atmosphere that encompasses all these dynamics and a host of others as well. We appear calm and confident. We may even *feel* calm and confident—for a little while. There is an electricity in the air. We are moving around in the pursuit of accomplishing that day's prescribed achievements. We have a purpose. We have a goal. There is a likeness of spirit with those around us. We are a part of a much bigger picture that will change or improve our society. It is exciting.

Or is it? The electricity in the air may be a result of tension. Our movement may be a drive to achieve an unattainable goal. The likeness of spirit may be undermined by conflict. We may not see any changes at all in society as a result of our efforts. What was once exciting may soon become stressful.

If we felt tremendous stress in our homes, we would probably be actively seeking relief. In the office place, however, we focus on the problems directly related to the business. If there is stress, how does that affect our work performance? The focus is usually not on the relationships of the personalities involved. It may not even be practical to give a lot of time to personalities.

Awareness of the unique atmosphere of the office can help to prevent inappropriate relationships. What we take so much for granted is really an arena of potential conflict. The mixed bag of excitement and stress can easily make the office a fertile field for vulnerability.

Just to be aware of that fact—that where you spend at least one third of your time is a place of potential vulnerability—can help you to be prepared for attacks in your areas of weakness. The atmosphere of the working world will not change. There will always be a combination of excitement and pressure. It is dangerous to think of the work place as just another place where we spend some time. It is a major part of our lives and has some inherent qualities that do not exist elsewhere.

Besides, immorality is exciting. That doesn't sound like a "Christian" statement, but it is. Sin is fun. That is part of Satan's way of entangling believers in his trap. The exciting atmosphere in the office can fan the spark between two people into a flame. In the secular office place, immorality is not the issue; getting the work of the company done is what matters. Usually, professional behavior is expected, but what is happening behind the scenes (or closed doors) is often of little concern.

The cumulative effects of office pressure are also conducive to immoral relationships. People in a similar situation under similar pressures are drawn together for reinforcement. If unprepared, an adulterous relationship can develop rapidly as a result of pressure.

The trappings of the professional world are many: cocktail parties, business lunches, late night meetings, weekend conferences, powerful people doing powerful things—and "doing your own thing" is part of the package. It is unlikely that we can move out of that atmosphere totally, but we can learn to be aware of its pitfalls and stand against them.

Competition

There is an atmosphere of inner-office competition. There may be some competitiveness that exists in the home, but hopefully not to the degree that it does in the work place.

Because of this competition, we are "on" when in the office. Or at least we *appear* to be on. Since work is a livelihood and the loss of work is a threat, we compete seriously. Competition creates comparison. Comparison may result in fear of being less competent than someone else. Feelings of inadequacy put us again in an arena of vulnerability.

When we feel inadequate, we may seek a feeling of significance in the wrong place. We can always find someone we work with who is sympathetic. But a relationship based on need for comfort and sympathy can be a dangerous one.

It is important to compare ourselves with biblical standards and not with other people. Nice statement. Awfully tough one to live out in an office. We need to understand what is expected of us from our superiors—and what the Lord expects. Then we need to operate with integrity and diligence and not with an attitude of constantly looking around at what others are doing.

Because most businesses do not operate by biblical standards, this criterion may be hard to determine. In fact, many businesses operate against biblical principles. Thus, when we feel threatened because of feelings of inadequacy, we need to be on guard as to where we turn for comfort.

Unlimited time, limited relationships

We often hear a woman say that her husband's secretary spends more time with him than she does. That is probably true. People in work relationships spend a great deal of time together. Often we are required to work longer than eight-hour days. Even if we only work a traditional eight hours, that is still a lot of time spent together.

We are also encouraged in this age of communication to be "open" with other people. Openness in a healthy way is certainly a positive element in any relationship. Unlimited openness, however, is not healthy.

The combination of long hours spent together and the encouragement of openness can be risky if we are not prepared for that risk. Extensive time and open communication together encourage closeness. All that sounds good. Certainly the Lord wants us to be close to others. The problem is the way in which we are close.

Listen to the ingredients: a man and a woman, a lot of time spent together, open communication, closeness. What is the obvious potential?

Does this mean that we cannot spend time in open communication with someone we work with? It depends. It depends on how we feel, how the other person feels, and how we interact together. If there is a "chemistry," then great limits have to be placed on all three elements. If there is legitimate friendship (nothing at all immoral in desires or actions), then there can be time, communication, and closeness. *Limited.* Limited time, limited communication, and limited closeness. We simply cannot have unlimited relationships with members of the opposite sex and expect to have controlled relationships.

But what kind of limits? In work relationships, time should be structured around the need to accomplish the work. To fill a lot of time with long meals and idle conversation can be a danger sign. Conversation should not be provocative. Provocative is anything that stirs up the other person—or yourself. It is inappropriate to listen to complaints about someone's wife or husband. It is also inappropriate to discuss dating frustrations if you are single in other than very general terms. We even need to exercise discretion when discussing something as seemingly harmless as a movie we have seen or a book we have read.

This may sound narrow. But the effects of provocative conversation are teasers. They plant a seed of "teasing with sin" in the minds of the parties involved.

If you are spending a lot of time with someone, you need to honestly evaluate your thinking about that person. You need to look at him with regard to your marriage as well. Do you think more often of him than of your spouse? Do you value his opinion more than that of your spouse, even if neither he nor your spouse knows that? If you have an opportunity to either be with that person or be at home, do you lean toward being with that person? Any of these areas are danger signs.

If you do have a relationship that is heading toward "risky," the time spent with that person may have to change. Work may not appear to permit that change. But personal integrity and family relationships are more important than any job. Look seriously at a way to change the time spent with that other person.

Common interests

It is very exciting and rewarding to be with someone who has the same interests you have. When a job is not a job but a passion, being involved in it makes the heart beat fast and the imagination leap at the possibilities of success.

This may be especially true in Christian work. Unusual levels of commitment and dedication are often required of the worker in a Christian ministry. The rewards are not monetary, but appeal to your sense of duty and service. Because of this "higher calling" dimension, there is great emotion tied into the work.

In the secular marketplace, the common interest may be based on different values—money, achievement—but the result is the same. Common interests encourage close relationships.

Again, this is not wrong in and of itself. What is wrong is to be unaware of the potential danger in a relationship with the emotional dimension of "playing on the same team." In Chapter 27, we will look at how to have healthy relationships with members of the opposite sex. Some of the most rewarding and healthy relationships exist in the framework of shared goals. But these relationships cannot be healthy if immorality is present.

To help prevent immorality, you must be aware that shared

interests can be conducive to closeness. Strive to keep the closeness right before the Lord and not unhealthy.

Manipulation

As a believer you may have to suffer persecution in the work place because of your unwillingness to succumb to sexual manipulation. In this day of women's rights, we don't hear too much of office manipulation by the means of sexual pressure. But it still exists. It may not be as blatant as the style depicted in movies: the young starlet back in the 1940s allowing herself to be seduced by the powerful producer in order to land a leading role in a movie. But the game still goes on.

Saying no to unwanted advances may result in some stress at work. The Bible refers to this as being persecuted for righteousness' sake. In 1 Peter 2:20 we read, "How is it to your credit if you receive a beating for doing wrong and endure it? But if you suffer for doing good and you endure it, this is commendable before God."

If someone in authority over you makes an advance and you turn him down, he may resort to manipulation. He may make your life miserable. This is not always a situation with a man in authority above a woman. Women may be the ones making the advances, too.

If a job situation becomes unfair due to taking a moral stand, hang in there with your integrity, or look for another job. It is often not that cut and dried, but the bottom line is that your integrity is more important than the job.

A word to the homemaker

What does all this mean to the woman who is at home all day?

Be aware. Realize that your husband enters a world every day that has its own set of temptations and challenges. He is bombarded with philosophies of the world. He is surrounded by women who are dressed to the teeth, aggressive, and looking at him in a different way than you are.

Not all women in the working world are this way. But be aware that the world he enters from nine to five has that element as one of its components.

Also, be concerned about your appearance, your attitude, your interests in his work, your knowledge of what is going on in the world. You are in competition. He may be the most faithful man in the world, but he is assaulted. Help him by helping yourself be all that he needs in a wife—not perfect, but trying to meet his needs and helping protect him from temptations.

The man married to a working woman

In many Christian families today, the woman works. The husband and wife both leave in the morning and go to the office arena. They both become frazzled from the same frustrations of work, temptation, family.

The man who is married to a working woman needs to realize that she is facing the same challenges that he is in his office. The old perspective that men are the only ones facing sexual temptations is gone. A woman in the work force is constantly around men who are "on the prowl." She relates daily to the aggressive, suave "mover." She, too, needs the emotional protection that her husband can help provide. She needs the same concern and care that the man returning home from work needs.

The center of the home

Whether you are married or single, male or female, working or at home, the ultimate source of security and significance is in the Lord. We have a responsibility as believers to relate to others in ways that minister to them. But the final, core source of fulfillment is in your relationship with Jesus Christ.

Other people can help in the battle against immorality. They, however, will be rendered powerless in the face of heated battle unless you have a firm relationship with the Lord at the center of your life.

SEVENTEEN

Professional Behavior

The next time you pass a secular bookstore, stop for a moment and browse through the business section. You will find books on how to dress for success, how to talk to intimidate, how to have body language that communicates confidence, how to manage to maximize, how to learn to do anything you need to do in order to succeed.

As Christians, how do we take all the "how tos" and integrate them into a biblical lifestyle? It is confusing. It requires being exposed to two distinctly different mind-sets, and continually choosing to operate based on one while being heavily subjected to the other.

Immorality as viewed from a worldly perspective

Recently there has been a slight shift in the world's view of immorality. Political scandals, evangelical scandals, and AIDS have contributed to this changing perspective. For many years previously, the world's view of immorality has been "do your own thing." That is still a predominant school of thought. But, there is a new dimension entering the picture. People are concerned about how their leaders can be honest in political affairs if they are dishonest in personal ones. And the health risks of promiscuity are dramatically affecting lifestyles.

In May of 1982, Chuck Colson said, "If you follow daily headlines you will quickly conclude that the dominant issues in American society are inflation and economic policy, or defense spending and social security, or conflicts between conservative and liberal political philosophies. But these are surface issues. The deeper issues are first, what values will we live by—absolute truth, the Holy Word of God, or the arbitrary, relative whims of the humanist elite; and second, who will set the moral agenda—the church or the bureaucratic social planners and vested economic interests of secular society?"[9]

We are gradually moving into the area of those deeper issues. It has been over five years since Mr. Colson made those statements—and our headlines are now constantly focused on the morality of political candidates, the scandal of infidelity in the evangelical community, and the price being paid for illicit sex. The motives of the interest in these issues may not be godly, but the result is that the world is at least looking at issues that Christians have always been concerned with.

To live a sexually moral life in order to prevent a deadly disease should not be the primary reason one seeks that lifestyle, but AIDS has nevertheless thrown a biblical issue into the spotlight. A resulting lifestyle change in favor of morality would certainly help everyone, including Christians, to more successfully live a godly life.

In the August 1987 issue of *Life* magazine, an article was published called "Sex and the Presidency." This article was a result of the publicity given Gary Hart, who had been the Democratic presidential front runner up to that point. But after being seen with a single young woman while he was staying at his Washington townhouse, the news media widely circulated the story of a sex scandal, ending Hart's campaign. Suddenly a media blitz was launched on the issue of the importance of sexual morality.

The *Life* article stated, "When it comes to their President, Americans agree on one thing: He is a moral symbol for our nation. Seventy-one percent believe that he should be held to a higher standard of morality than other Americans. There is surprising disagreement, however, on what constitutes morality. Almost half feel that marital infidelity has nothing to do with a person's qualifications for President. One third regard adultery as unpardonable, disqualifying a person for the job. . . . What appears most crucial to voters is honesty."[10]

There is a distinction, apparently, between sexual morality and nonsexual morality (such as integrity, honesty, discretion). The implication does exist, however, that if a man is sexually immoral *and* presents an image contrary to that fact, he is suspect.

The article went on to say that "some of these candidates would be much better off to divorce rather than to play that they are happily married." Fifty-two percent of the people polled also felt that "a President with loose personal morals is more likely to carry that behavior into public office. 'If he's not faithful to his wife,' one woman says, 'he won't be faithful to the country.'"[10]

American public opinion seems to be tottering between maintaining attitudes of both "do your own thing" and "don't do your own thing if it affects me." We can bring that right down to personal relationships. The world says it's okay to live and let live. But what happens when that philosophy hits close to home? How does a wife feel when she learns that *her* husband is involved with another woman? How does a man feel when *his* wife wants a divorce to marry someone else? A person doesn't have to run for the presidency to be dubbed immoral when his actions affect us personally.

The world's view of morality is being challenged. It is under the spotlight from the intimacy of our homes to the public arena of the White House.

What does this mean for the believer in the work place?
Christians are under greater scrutiny than ever before. People are on the lookout for hypocrisy. If you claim to be a Christian, your lifestyle better match up with your profession—or someone will call attention to your double life.

But this is all good news. We *should* be living godly lives motivated by our love for the Lord. Since we have little support from the world in doing that, it is good for the world to hold us accountable for living what we preach.

It is important that we project an image consistent with our testimony. If we are Christians, then we are called to be open Christians. "Go into all the world and preach the good news" is the command (Mark 16:15). We don't have to be missionaries in a foreign country to be in the world preaching the good news of the gospel.

We "preach the gospel" every day at work. By our words and actions, we tell people what we believe. Christians are to be like Christ. That means we are to be like Him at work, as well as at home or in church.

Professional dress, talk, demeanor

We can go back to the secular bookstore to find out how to dress for success. But what about how to dress to project an image of godliness? Actually, professional "success" dress is pretty much in line with appropriate dress for the Christian.

Gone are the days of the miniskirt in the office. Nehru jackets and gold chains are a thing of the past, as well. Conservative dress is the prescription for the corporate ladder climber.

For the Christian, we are to be modest, not drawing attention to ourselves. In women's clothes, it is obvious what that means. Dresses that are too short or too low-cut are not an appropriate reflection of a life committed to the Lord. There is little conflict with the world here because the dress for women in the office, at least for the time being, is appropriately conservative.

Men have traditionally been conservative dressers in the corporate world. What, then, is inappropriate for the Christian businessman? Again, anything that draws undue attention to the person. There is a great deal of controversy over "Rolex" versus "Timex." A statement is made by both. Each person will have to decide for himself what he is saying by any particular item he chooses to wear. It is not wrong to wear something that obviously costs a lot of money, any more than it is wrong to wear something functional but low in cost. What is important is, What are you saying about yourself?

The way we talk says a great deal about our values. Coarse talk is common in the world, but has no place in the vocabulary of the Christian. Ephesians 5:4 says, "Nor should there be obscenity, foolish talk or coarse joking, which are out of place, but rather thanksgiving."

I remember my freshman year at college—back in the dark ages—I had not been used to being around girls who used coarse language. In fact, the boys I had known did not use coarse language in front of girls. College was different. The first week, my ears were burning from the expletives of the girls in the dorm. Soon, however, I got used to their talk. I never picked it up personally, but I got so used to it that it did not shock me to hear it.

Picking up bad habits is easy to do in a work situation, too. After a lot of exposure to something, we become used to it and it no longer offends us. It may even become part of our behavior. We need to be careful, to be on the alert to things that are offensive to the Lord and that do not reflect His image in our lives.

Inappropriate dress and provocative talk invite immoral overtures. They say to others that we may be open to other areas of inconsistency in our Christian lives. It may be that we are *not* open, but these actions imply it nevertheless.

More important than any single factor of our behavior is our overall demeanor. The whole package. What kind of statement do you make when you walk into a room? What does a person observing you conclude without even speaking to you? What three words would coworkers use to describe you to someone who had never met you? Would anyone be able to tell that you are a Christian by the way you look, talk, and act?

I spoke recently with a committed Christian man who is in a prominent position with a major corporation. He talked of how provocative some of the women in his office are. He is happily married and is an outspoken believer. But that does not stop some inappropriate behavior by his coworkers. Their "demeanor" invites immorality.

He described how, just that morning, he was by the copy machine when a woman in the office came up next to him and leaned against him. She didn't say anything unusual—but she lingered next to him provocatively. He went directly into his office, not responding at all to her manner.

Often sexually manipulative behavior may say just the opposite of the obvious. "A woman's resistance is no proof of her virtue: it is much more likely to be a proof of her experience. If we spoke sincerely, we should have to confess that our first impulse is to yield; we only resist on reflection."[11] But one's "demeanor" can certainly be detected, especially if we work with someone over a long period of time. Resistance can often be flirtatious and teasing, but that, too, can be determined by the overall manner of the person.

Professional behavior demands nonparticipation in office game playing. Leaning up against a person and acting like you don't know you're doing it is out. The Christian has a responsibility to send out consistent signals.

Claiming to be a Christian who lives a moral lifestyle and then subtly acting provocative is dishonest, unfair, and ungodly. A Christian in the office place, or anywhere, should reflect the characteristics of Jesus Christ. We need to be willing to suffer criticism or ridicule because of our moral stand.

The Christian woman in the office

All of this does not mean that we have to be a stick-in-the-mud. We should also reflect joy. So, what *do* we do? As Christian women we establish our actions, words, the whole package, based on the Word of God. We can be modest without being drab. We can be fun without being coarse. We can be accepting of others without responding to inappropriate advances.

Chances are that if we establish our standards from the first day on the job, we will have little trouble with pushy men. Sometimes, a godly stand will draw out a challenge. Someone may set out to break down our resistance. But, if we are firm from the start, attention will be turned elsewhere.

I enjoy being a very outgoing person. That is my personality. But it is often misread—at first. My friendliness and sense of humor may seem to someone who does not know me as an invitation. I establish early on by what I say and the way I say it—sincerely and not teasing in any way—that I am a committed Christian. That is usually enough to deter any unwanted interest. Chapter 21 includes other specific behavior to help us stay on track.

Here are a few suggestions to project a positive, fun demeanor without being a tease:

- Care about your appearance. Be neat and clean, with nails groomed and hair immaculate.
- Smile. Listen attentively without sending out lingering glances.
- Ask people questions about themselves that show you care about them, but not provocative questions.
- Don't be involved in gossip.
- Don't be critical.
- Learn to look at others as you think Christ looks at them.
- Pray for opportunities to be a witness for Him.

Christian men at work

What has been said about women in the office also holds true for men. I would like to include a list of "rules" that Jerry Jenkins wrote in his column in *Moody Monthly*. Jerry emphasizes that these "rules" are really just hedges that he builds around himself to protect himself, his wife, his family, his employer, his church, and the reputation of Christ:

> 1. Whenever I need to meet or dine or travel with an unrelated woman, I make it a threesome. Should an unavoidable last-minute complication make this impossible, my wife hears it from me first.
>
> 2. I am careful about touching. While I might shake hands or squeeze an arm or shoulder in greeting, I embrace only dear friends or relatives, and only in front of others.
>
> 3. If I pay a compliment, it is on clothes or hairstyle, not on the person herself. Commenting on a pretty outfit is much different, in my opinion, than telling a woman that she herself looks pretty.
>
> 4. I avoid flirtation or suggestive conversation, even in jest.
>
> 5. I remind my wife often in writing and orally that I remember my wedding vows: "Keeping you only unto me for as long as we both shall live. . . ." Dianna is not the jealous type, nor has she ever demanded such assurances from me. She does, however, appreciate my rules and my observance of them.
>
> 6. From the time I get home from work until the children go to bed, I do no writing or office work. This gives me lots of time with the family and for my wife and me to continue to court and date.[12]

I had the opportunity to personally meet Jerry Jenkins in 1980 at a writer's conference. He was then with *Moody Monthly* and is now Vice President for Publishing for Moody Bible Institute. We discussed the possibility of doing a book: He would have helped me write my testimony about my husband's death. We did not end up doing the book, but something happened then that I recalled when reading Jerry's list of guidelines.

I was in the Chicago area and had planned to meet Jerry at his office to discuss the potential book. My plans were delayed and I arrived in downtown Chicago around dinner time instead of in the afternoon. Jerry, instead of staying in town for dinner, invited me to his home for dinner. I had the opportunity to meet Dianna and their children and have a very enjoyable evening in a family setting. I didn't know then, and don't know now if Jerry often does that. But I do know that it was a very nice and appropriate meeting.

This is not to say that to meet for dinner in a restaurant is wrong. I am simply saying that there can be alternatives that we sometimes don't take advantage of. I appreciated seeing a business contact in the context of his home and in a way that allowed for a very comfortable friendship to exist between us.

Special temptations while traveling

While the office is a unique arena of temptation, the "travel scene" is like a hot fudge sundae to the dieter. The primary danger in maintaining a moral lifestyle while traveling is that there is no accountability. And, we are around other people with no accountability.

We can tend to feel like "little islands" when away from home. Hotels are full of business travelers who are there for a night and gone. The loneliness of travel draws people together. Flying alone, dining alone, stressful meetings, and—alone again. The scene is set for temptation.

Hotels have an atmosphere of intrigue and romance—from the HBO in the rooms, to the torch songs floating out from the lounge. One somehow expects to hear Humphrey Bogart whisper, "Play it again, Sam."

Travel places one in a vulnerable position. Weariness, loneliness, seductive surroundings. All of them contribute to being vulnerable to temptations of immorality.

Being aware of the temptations ahead of time is a beginning. We need to determine that our behavior will not invite any of those temptations. Women need only to walk in a certain way from the front desk to the elevator to elicit approaches. Men need only to stare appreciatively to be noticed.

The overall demeanor is the same as in the office—but more so. It is possible to be warm and friendly without being provocative. It is even more essential while traveling to be cautious in the signals we send out, because we do not know the people we are around. A little tease that would be practically ignored in the office could produce big trouble away from home.

We go continually back to the reflection of the character of Jesus

Christ. He traveled the highways of His world, always projecting a consistent image. We will not reach His perfection, but we have an opportunity to strive toward His example.

PART VI

Relationships Between Singles

EIGHTEEN

Godly Dating

Evaluate where you are.

The first thing to do is to evaluate your relationship with Jesus Christ. Is He first in your list of priorities, or are you hoping for a special someone to come along to answer all your needs?

Maybe the Lord is saying that you need to work on your relationship with Him and that perhaps you need to wait a while to enter another relationship. Or perhaps you have not given yourself enough time to heal from a past hurt. If you are hoping for a new relationship to take away the pain of an old one, chances are you need to wait before becoming involved again. Allow Christ to heal you. Don't depend on another person to do it.

When you are secure in your relationship with the Lord—aware that He alone can meet your deep needs and trusting in Him to do just that—then you may be ready to take the risk of beginning a dating relationship.

Decide your behavior before involvement.

What are your personal standards for a dating relationship? Have you even established any specific ones? If you don't have some guidelines established ahead of time, it may be difficult to start them after you get emotionally involved.

Each of us must examine his or her own heart before the Lord. We must be willing to submit to what He dictates. Once again, the key is to put the relationship with Him first. Then we will see more clearly what is acceptable and what is not.

If our relationship with the Lord is not our top priority as it needs to be, we are in great danger of slipping below any biblical standard of moral conduct. The temptations of the flesh are too strong to be combatted with a list of "do nots." The stronger the relationship with the Lord before we begin dating, the better we will be able to see clearly that moral purity is a blessing meant for our protection.

Much has been written about the physical limitations Christians should adhere to when dating. You can read advice covering the whole gamut from absolutely no physical contact to what is referred to as "responsible petting." There is universal agreement among Christians that sexual intercourse is always wrong outside of marriage. The biblical standard, of course, is that sexual contact and fulfillment must be limited to marriage.

There are no pat answers. Some people can enjoy some physical contact and not be stirred to a point where they will lose control. A kiss may be a warm, affectionate expression of love and caring. For others, a kiss is the beginning of a fire that they may not be able to control.

Once again, rationalization can be a danger. We may justify considerable sexual contact because we are going to marry the person. Or we think we can become involved to a deeper level physically because we love the other person. But do these things make it right?

Right behavior before the Lord is moral purity. Biblical moral purity means that sexual activities are limited to the arena of marriage. A person must decide for himself or herself what specific activities are sexually provocative. Is kissing okay? Is a little more than kissing okay? Is no contact at all the only appropriate behavior?

Why not simply state what God's standard is? Because I believe that the central issue is our relationship with Him. If that is being wholeheartedly pursued, godly relationships will be a byproduct. This may seem like mental gymnastics, but I think the distinction is important. If we have a list to live by, we can easily change or justify that list when temptation arises. If, on the other hand, we have a valid relationship with the living God and we seek first to please Him, we will have more motivation to live a pure life.

There is an old saying, "When in doubt, don't." As a *genuine* relationship with Christ grows, so does one's discernment. When we walk in spiritual unity with the Lord, we experience a sense of His pleasure. The more we walk with Him, the more we become aware of the security that we are in the center of His will. In the same way, when we begin to falter, we will sense His displeasure.

If you begin to feel an uneasiness creeping into your dating situation, look closely to see if there is any *behavior* that may be displeasing to the Lord. Sometimes we call this "conscience." I prefer the word "discernment." If you discern some unrest—that something is not quite right—you should be open to the possibility that you are displeasing the Lord.

A telltale indicator of too much physical involvement is justification. "We aren't hurting anyone"; "It wasn't too much involvement, so it was okay"; "It only happens once in a while." When these kinds of rationalizations slip in, watch out. When in doubt, *don't.*

The complexities of adult dating

Even as adults, our emotions still behave much as if we were still teenagers. We need to be aware that although we may feel like we did at sixteen, we now face many issues we didn't as teens.

Very often there are ex-spouses, children, and two whole lifetimes of different experiences between two dating adults. If you have been alone for any length of time, there is also a sense of independence that now clashes with another person's independence.

As we enter dating relationships, we need to determine what we are willing to change and what we are not. If we marry at twenty-five, there aren't many habits that need changing. At forty-five, there are years of establishing certain habit patterns that now suit us, and we may not be as willing to change. This can cause problems in dating.

Time

You may sometimes feel that you are running out of time because of your age. I know young girls in their twenties who are panicking at the thought of entering their thirties without a mate. I can relate to them as I move into my forties without being remarried. Again, age is no reason to have an immoral relationship just so the man may marry you.

It is important to realize that no matter how old you may be, you have all the time you need. Your time is in the hands of the Lord. You need not rush ahead on some manmade deadline.

The flip side of this coin is to recognize when time is no longer a factor. I have known some couples who have dated for several years. They keep talking about marriage, but never make the step. The familiarity of such close relationships could easily slip into immorality.

We live in a "couples" society.

To further complicate the already difficult struggle to maintain a biblical morality, our society reinforces a "couples" world: If you are normal, you are part of a "couple." According to these standards, it certainly doesn't matter if you are married or not, or even if it is a man and a woman who comprise the couple. A large part of a person's identity is just to be going with someone.

In the Christian world, the implications of this mentality are strongly felt. There is an underlying insinuation that if you aren't dating, there is something wrong with you.

A Christian man, forty-five and divorced, once told me he had a book for me to read on why women my age are afraid of sex. His answer for my moral stand was that there was something sexually wrong with me. His attitude was that it wasn't realistic to think that believers our age could date and not have sex. He felt the Bible was practical in every way except on the issue of premarital sex.

Another incident, thrown out of proportion because of my non-couple status, angered and insulted me. I have a close friendship with a divorced woman who is also a committed Christian. She seldom dates, but when she does, she maintains a biblically moral lifestyle. A male acquaintance of hers, who couldn't comprehend her stand, took great pleasure in making cutting remarks that implied that she and I were romantically involved with each other.

The "only human" side of me wanted to take this man and choke him. His perverted attitude required that everyone had to be involved sexually and physically—even if that involvement were a perversion. It made more sense to him that my friend and I would be involved with each other than with no one.

Another wrong response I had to his accusation was the thought of getting quickly involved with a man to validate my "normalness." But I quickly came to my senses and realized that my first responsibility was to Christ, not to this man in particular or to society in general.

A Relationship with Christ

A close relationship with Christ must be the priority of your life. There will be a tremendous temptation to continually daydream about your new relationship with another person. I know this one well because I do it well. My mind can be almost totally consumed with thoughts of how to please, how to improve myself, how to be more feminine, etc.—which takes up a lot of energy and diverts my attention away from the Lord.

But keep the Lord first. Keep Him first because it pleases Him, because it is the obedient thing to do. Keep Him first because He will bless your new relationships as a result.

Dating in a godly fashion is an enormous challenge. You will often feel like the Lone Ranger. There is much compromise in this area of the Christian community. Decide today to be different. Decide to make your life before the Lord conform to Scripture, not to the standards of the day.

If this area of your life is ungodly, you cannot expect to be blessed in other areas. As committed Christians, we simply cannot afford to let this dating standard slide. The move from "thoughts" to "involvement" happens all too quickly.

NINETEEN

A New Self-Image for the Single Believer

We constantly put people in boxes. For example:

Are you married or single?
Are you an outgoing temperament or a quiet temperament?
Are you a "dominant initiator" or a "responder"?
Are your colors "summer," "fall," "winter," or "spring"?
Are you conservative or liberal?
Are you up or down, in or out?

The result of labels

There can be some positive benefits as a result of better understanding yourself in terms of your temperament. It can be fun to know what colors look best on you. In the work arena, you may be able to improve your working relationships by better understanding your leadership style. And, doctrinally, we all tend to align ourselves with a church that adheres to familiar interpretations of Scripture.

But what kind of emphasis should we and other people put on our marital status? How should we respond when someone makes more than a passing comment on whether we are married or single?

Labeling or categorizing people leads to a preoccupation with self. One reason why I am not a particular fan of singles Sunday school classes is that often all those people with the same "problem" or "situation" go to the same class and discuss what's wrong with them. I have seen the result on many a single person. I have been in classes where it is announced that so-and-so has "graduated" from the class and is getting married. What a loaded statement—with such disparaging connotations! No wonder there is a poor self-image established when a person concludes that the only way to advance is to get married.

Marital status, of course, *greatly* affects our lives, roles, responsibilities, and image of ourselves. But our error is when the view of self becomes negative because of singleness. Paul was a strong proponent of the single state, and there are numerous others. Their singleness did not, however, determine their self-worth. Neither did the married status of others determine their self-worth.

What has happened?

Most of us live in a "couples" society. Our society evaluates people based on a number of criteria, including with whom they are coupled.

If you're single and not dating at all, there's an unspoken attitude of "What's wrong with you?" When enough people start asking you why you aren't married, you may find yourself asking the same question: "Why am I not married?" The answer may reflect deep feelings of inadequacy.

If, on the other hand, you are single and dating, then who you date becomes the focus. The typical questions asked are, "What does he (or she) do for a living?" and, "Is he (or she) a Christian?" Women ask other women what he looks like, and I would assume that men ask men the same thing. All of this is normal, but unfortunately the emphasis is on the externals. I include asking if a person is a Christian as an external because many people profess to be Christians whose walk with the Lord does not reflect a mature level of commitment.

Our value system has fallen into line with that of the world. If you are alone, there must be something wrong. If you are with someone, it needs to be someone that the world would deem successful.

Our images tend to come from role models. In most churches today, it is difficult to find godly role models who are single believers. Leadership in churches is generally occupied by married believers. That's okay. We don't want to qualify people based on their marital status at all, so married is as good as single. But there just aren't many singles in leadership roles. There are more within the singles ministries of churches, but, again, that's usually *because* they are single.

There is also the controversial issue of whether a divorced

person should be in a leadership position at all. If people are prohibited from leadership because of divorce, they still have the opportunity to be a role model by virtue of their relationship with the Lord.

Somehow, we need to come to the point of viewing ourselves as whole and complete people based on our relationship with Christ and not our marital status.

Women: world model, biblical model, and church model

The world's model for the single woman is quite a package to live up to. She possesses a combination of good looks, brains, charm, assertiveness, independence, and savoir-faire. If you think I am exaggerating, go to a secular bookstore and look at the business section. Many of the books address women. Most of them are on how to be the model of "everything" all wrapped in one well-organized package. Granted, not all the women are presumed to be single. But most single women are working women, and so this is the information passed on to all working women today: Be brilliant.

The image of the worldly woman when it comes to sex is someone who is sure she is practicing "safe" sex. Because of AIDS, we are no longer encouraged to be recklessly promiscuous, but rather "safely" promiscuous. The result may be a higher moral standard. But the motive is not one based on a relationship with God. It is based on how to still have premarital sex without getting deathly ill. If I were to describe the world's image of a single woman in one word, it would be "smart." She is to project an image of clever awareness, adeptly dealing with a dangerous world in a clever way. How opposite of being "wise." How opposite of being feminine in a godly way.

What about biblical role models of single women? Mary and Martha were sisters from Bethany. We read of Mary pouring perfume on the Lord and wiping His feet with her hair. We see the two sisters as they interact with Jesus at the death—and resurrection—of their brother, Lazarus.

Mary and Martha believed in Christ. Here is an example of Martha's faith in action:

> "Lord," Martha said to Jesus, "if you had been here, my brother would not have died. But I know that even now God will give you whatever you ask. . . ."

> Jesus said to her, "I am the resurrection and the life. He who believes in me will live, even though he dies; and whoever lives and believes in me will never die. Do you believe this?"
>
> "Yes, Lord," she told him, "I believe that you are the Christ, the Son of God, who was to come into the world." (John 11:21-27)

Mary and Martha were women of faith. It did not matter if they were married or not. If they had been married, the account might only have been different by describing them by their name and the name of their husbands. None of their personal qualities were based on their marital status. Their character is described in Scripture by their relationship to the Lord.

Many other women played key roles in Jesus' ministry:

> Jesus traveled about from one town and village to another, proclaiming the good news of the kingdom of God. The Twelve were with him, and also some women who had been cured of evil spirits and diseases: Mary (called Magdalene) from whom seven demons had come out; Joanna the wife of Cuza, the manager of Herod's household; Susanna; and many others. These women were helping to support them out of their own means." (Luke 8:1-3)

Joanna was married, and the others were not. It was of no issue whether they were married or not. The only thing common among these women was that they were helping to support Jesus and His disciples out of their own means.

Paul on his visit to Philippi met Lydia, who proved to be another woman of faith:

> One of those listening was a woman named Lydia, a dealer in purple cloth from the city of Thyatira, who was a worshiper of God. The Lord opened her heart to respond to Paul's message. When she and the members of her household were baptized, she invited us to her home. "If you consider me a believer in the Lord," she said, "come and stay at my house." And she persuaded us. (Acts 16:14-15)

Paul and Silas indeed returned to Lydia's house to meet with other believers.

In Romans 16:1-16, we see that Paul sent greetings to a number of people. Many of them were women, none of them mentioned by marital status.

When the Bible mentions women (and men), it identifies them by their relationship to the Lord or to the apostles. It talks of their hearts or their ministries. A woman was often mentioned as the wife of her husband, as was the custom of the day. We still do that today: "Mrs." followed by her husband's first and last names. It did not then, nor should it now, denote anything specific about the woman's character or worth.

I am not making a case here for the role of women in leadership. I *am* pointing out that when women were mentioned in Scripture, it was not emphasized whether they were married or not. They were not complete or incomplete based on whether or not they were married.

Contemporary churches have a role model for the Christian woman that is almost always presented as that of wife and mother. They consider the classic Scripture passage on women to be Proverbs 31, which describes a woman who is married and has a family. But where does all this leave the single woman?

In Isaiah 54:5, we read, "For your Maker is your husband—the LORD Almighty is his name—the Holy One of Israel is your Redeemer; he is called the God of all the earth." What a full life for the woman who takes the characteristics of the woman in Proverbs 31 and applies them to a relationship with the Lord! As for having children, there is such a crying need for spiritual mothers (and fathers) within the Church that the single woman need never look far for someone to nurture.

We need to turn a deaf ear to teaching that suggests that a woman is not complete without a husband. We need to turn to the Lord and His Word, and find that total completeness is possible with or without a man. At the end of this chapter, we will look at how we should balance the desires of wanting to be married with the reality of being single.

What about the account of Creation where God brings woman into existence to be a partner with man? How does this square with Paul's statement in 1 Corinthians 7:8? "Now to the unmarried and the widows I say: It is good for them to stay unmarried, as I am. But if they cannot control themselves, they should marry. . . ." What happened between Genesis and 1 Corinthians? What God intended for Adam and Eve was tarnished by the Fall. Because of that earliest sin, we live in a world that will always struggle with proper relationships. None of us, married or single, experience the perfection that God originally intended.

So, the issue is not whether we should marry or not, but that we should live obediently. Obedience includes living a morally pure life. If we are single, we are called to live a life of chastity. If we are married, we are called to live faithfully with our mate.

Our wholeness and completeness before the Lord is not determined by marriage or singleness, but by a relationship with Him that puts Him first.

Adam was not worth less in the eyes of God without his wife, Eve. The faithful women mentioned in many passages of Scripture were not worth less in the eyes of God because they were single. Our worth is established with God—not because of anything in us, but by His Son.

Our self-image, our self-worth, should not be dependent on our status in this world, but only on our intimate relationship with Jesus Christ.

To have a godly estimate of ourselves does not mean that we will *feel* happy all the time about whether we are married or not. It does mean that we can become aware that we are valuable people in God's eyes regardless of our marital status. In fact, the very fact that God did send Christ to intercede for us validates our worth in a way that no other means could accomplish.

Men: world model, biblical model, church model

The role model for men in the world is a real potpourri. While women are moving in the world from the kitchen to the boardroom, men are moving from the boardroom to the gay communities, to "do whatever you want, whenever you want, however you want."

The macho image still exists, but it is challenged daily. It depends on the circle in which you travel as to what is the ideal. Married or single seems almost totally irrelevant. Unlike women, men are not viewed as having something wrong with them if they are not married. Now if they are over forty and have *never* been married, then they may fall suspect to having some deficiency. Because homosexuality is now so commonly accepted, the never-married male is still more accepted than the never-married female.

Rather than by marital status, the world seems to judge men by the amassing of wealth. There is a popular slogan that says, "Whoever dies with the most toys wins." While the collecting of material things is the major preoccupation expressed in this slogan, there is also a sexual aspect to this lifestyle of hedonism.

Celibacy is not lifted up as a lifestyle for men in our culture. The world does not place worth on men according to their married or single status, but it does assume that some kind of sexual expression is being lived out. So, while the emphasis is not on the sexual habits of men, there is an assumption that unrestricted, but "safe" sexual conduct is occurring. The world simply does not understand a single man who does not engage in any kind of sexual activity—unless he is a monk.

As with women, the biblical model for men was based on their relationship with God, not their marital status. In Scripture, men are sometimes identified as being married, but that is never an issue in the description of their character. When Jesus was calling the disciples, He identified them by profession: fishermen, tax collector, etc. (Matthew 4:18, 9:9).

As already mentioned, Paul made a strong case for being single. He gave plenty of room, however, for the institution of marriage. Does the Genesis account mean that man is not complete without woman? God said that it was not good for man to be alone. Perhaps in most cases it is better for us to have the strength of two together—but it is not an issue in determining our self-image, or self-worth. A man who is unmarried is of great value to the Lord because of his relationship with Christ.

Men in church leadership are usually married. However, single men have an opportunity to display a godly role model by the visible evidence of their relationship with the Lord. A single Christian man who lives a celibate life can be a great encouragement to all the men around him, especially the single men. Because so few single male role models exist, there is a great need and opportunity for godly men to strive to be an example.

A biblical view for men and women today

Have you ever made any of these statements to yourself?

- "I will do this for the Lord—until I get married."
- "I want to get married, so I will do this ministry until the Lord brings someone along."
- "I'm not dating, so I know I must be doing something wrong."
- "Surely God intends me to be married."

Maybe God does intend for you to get married in the future. Maybe not. The focus is not whether He will bring someone along or not. The focus is what He wants you to do with your life for Him *now.* Not now until you get married, but now and until He changes what exists now.

Amy Carmichael was a missionary to Japan, China, Ceylon, and India. She happened to be single all her life. But that was certainly not the determining factor in her going to the mission field. In *A Chance to Die* by Elisabeth Elliot, we read, "Looking back after fifty years Amy declared that she was 'no more fit to be a Keswick missionary than a Skye terrier puppy.' That estimate never caused her to question her validity of the call—or, we may assume, the judgment of the One who issued it."[13]

Amy Carmichael did not become a missionary to foreign countries because she was single, or even because she was particularly qualified, but because she was *called.* True, she may not have gone if she had been married. But in either case, it would have been because God had called her.

We all have a calling before the Lord. If we fill our minds with thoughts of being married versus being single, chances are that we will never hear that call. We will become so preoccupied with ourselves and our wants that we will miss the call of the Lord. And to miss the call of the Lord means to miss the most rewarding and fulfilling life possible this side of heaven.

We need to determine our moral standards, put Christ first in our lives, and go on to pursue Him and what He wants of our lives. Our worth is not even based on our fruitfulness in ministry. Our fruitfulness is a reward for service to the Lord. Our true worth, once again, is in the Lord Jesus Christ alone.

But I want to be married

Suppose you have determined to live a godly life and are doing it. You are single and living morally, yet you still have the desire to get married. That's okay. The important thing is to realize that you are not living on hold until or if that happens. Let the Lord know your desire, and go on fully with your life as His man or woman. Nothing, not even marriage, guarantees happiness. The pursuit of happiness is the wrong pursuit. The pursuit of Jesus is the only road to take for the believer.

Be sure to evaluate yourself in the eyes of the Lord, not the eyes of the world. Your standards will be challenged; you will be made fun of; you will be tempted. But He is able to keep you strong.

And what happened to Amy Carmichael?

> Forty years later Amy described for one of her "children" a transaction that had taken place when she was alone in a cave in Arima. Having gone there to spend a day in solitude she faced with God feelings of fear about the future. Loneliness hovered like a spectre on the horizon. Things were all right at the moment, but could she endure years of being alone? The devil painted pictures of loneliness which were vivid to her many years later, and she turned to the Lord in desperation. What can I do, Lord? How can I go on to the end? His answer: "None of them that trust in Me shall be desolate."[14]

If you are a Christian single man or woman, see yourself as totally loved. See yourself as totally accepted. See yourself as worthwhile, someone with a mission. That mission may be as invisible as that of a prayer warrior or as noticeable as the developer of a ministry. It doesn't matter. What matters is that you become aware of the complete security and significance you have in your relationship with your Creator.

TWENTY

The Dating Single Parent

A few years ago, I spoke at a mother-daughter banquet on relationships. When I finished, a friend of mine who was in the audience came up. "You will never guess what impressed my daughter the most about your talk," she said.

I felt a sense of eager expectation as I asked her what it was.

"She thought it would be so neat to have a mother who dated."

Her response didn't quite live up to my expectation. I could tell that it didn't live up to what she had expected either.

Anyone who thinks it's *fun* to live with a dating adult hasn't lived with one. This situation barely existed a generation ago. It has its own set of challenges and implications with regard to morality.

In the past, adults presented moral standards to their children and the parents were in the position of already having lived through that particular time of life—dating. Now, it is common to see a household of two generations with all the members of that household dating. Parents who are dating not only have to teach about dating, but they have to live it out in front of their children. That isn't all bad. But it provides a challenging and unusual arena in which parent-child relationships must grow.

Parents of teenagers

If the situations that bring parents to the point of dating were not so tragic, the whole scenario would be humorous. I have two teenage daughters. They are self-professed experts on men of my age group.

Their image of the perfect male is well ingrained in their minds. They have teenage friends who find my dating situations of great interest.

In other words, a man I date doesn't stand a chance. At least, not at first. I remember an incident a few years ago that was typical of a first date. My older daughter was home and her boyfriend was over. My younger daughter was also home. They were all conveniently doing something in the kitchen. My date arrived and I brought him into the kitchen to meet the troops. They all smiled politely and looked angelic. We exchanged a few comments and then he and I left.

As we walked down the path to his car, I could just (mentally) hear the conversation in the kitchen. Unfortunately, this nice man was not exactly *au courant* in his wardrobe. He also didn't have the most current hairstyle. I knew he was doomed.

We went to a movie and came back to my house. As we came in the front door, I could hear the kids downstairs playing Ping-Pong. I stopped at the head of the stairs, with my date behind me, and called down, "Hey—I'm home!"

"*Say*—how was the *dude*?" came the bellowing voice of my daughter's boyfriend.

"The 'dude' is right behind me," I said with humor, hopefully.

Silence floated up the stairs, and the dude and I went to the kitchen for a soda. He did not seem bothered by the remark, and I was grateful that it had not been the all-too-common tag of "geek."

After he left, the kids quietly appeared from the family room.

"*Mom*—he isn't your type. Did you *see* his slacks? Polyester! And the haircut. No, Mom, not this one."

They had obviously evaluated the meaningful aspects of this man and had—scratched him off.

All they are expecting is a combination of Tom Selleck, John Elway, and Billy Graham—great looking, athletic, and a spiritual giant. I am sure the children of men have equally prestigious ideals for the women their fathers date.

The humorous side is minor compared to the real issues of a dating parent. Although I have not been the child in that situation, I can speculate with some degree of experience on the problems those children face.

The most obvious threat seems to be that of the relationship between the child and the parent. They have already been through the trauma of the death or divorce of a parent—and now they have to risk, or so it seems, losing the other parent. Fear can generate some strange behavior. Criticism, which I have already touched on in a lighthearted fashion, is one of the results of fear. If children can contribute to the parent seeing the undesirability of the "date," then their own position in the parent's life remains the same.

They may also feel a sense of protectiveness toward the parent. In a single-parent home, the children enter into a role not often occupied by the children of two-parent homes. They are "little adults" who have to shoulder a large part of the responsibility usually carried by the two parents together. When a new person enters the scene, that role is threatened. They also may feel protective of the parent with whom they have been sharing responsibility.

The person dating the single parent may also be subjected to a great deal of comparison. A mother may be dating because she no longer has a husband, but her children may still have a father. Or, if he is no longer living, they still have a memory of a father. A child may feel the pressure to be "disloyal" when a new person enters the scene. He or she may feel that it is important to be negative about this person in order to be faithful to the parent of that same sex.

A child of any age is unhappy about the breakup of his or her family. A person dating one of the parents is a visible indication that the reestablishment of that family unit is no longer an option. Children of a broken home may dream that their parents will reunite, but that dream is harder to perpetuate when the parents start to date.

In the case of a parent dying, the children may have a particularly close relationship with the surviving parent. After all, they have been through a tragedy together. They feel mutually protective and close. They have seen each other through hard times. They adjust to life without the deceased parent. When other men (or women in the case of widowers) come around, the protective atmosphere they are used to is threatened. Also, children tend to compare this new person to the memory—not the reality—of the deceased parent. No one can measure up to that image.

What about immorality?

If your children are in their teens, they are acutely aware of the sexual potential when their parent begins dating. They already know what the parent teaches, but they will be watching closely to see what the parent *lives.* Be careful not to perpetuate a double standard. Biblical morality is not defined by a person's age. If you compromise in your standards, it will be difficult to expect your children to hold to those standards you ask of them. Teens are in great need of godly role models. Dating may be an opportunity to exemplify something that is rarely lived out by their peers.

What to do

These suggestions are certainly not an exhaustive list. They do not guarantee smooth running relationships between teens and their dating parents. But, they may aid in the establishing of better relationships:

1. *Continue to assume the role of parent.* There are three of us in my household, and we all three date. Sometimes, I feel like a nineteen-year-old myself. The phone is always ringing; people are coming and going. The atmosphere is a little like that of the sorority house where I lived in college. So, I am sometimes treated like one of the girls. Sometimes that's okay. Sometimes it is not.

I have to be careful to maintain my place as head of the house and parent of my children. Things cannot always happen equally. While there is no double standard morally, there are some distinctions in other areas—areas such as curfews, time on the phone, and who sets these rules. I set them. I feel guilty on occasion, but then I remind myself that I am the parent. I may be in a dating situation somewhat similar to that of my daughters, but I am still the one responsible before God for our household.

2. *Communicate openly.* This one is hard to accomplish, but worth the continued effort. If you don't know what your children are thinking, it is hard to relieve their fears.

3. *Encourage expression of your children's feelings in appropriate ways.* Even if they have negative feelings, encourage them to express themselves. They may feel negative about someone. They may be very angry. Allow your son or daughter to express his or her anger when the two of you are alone. After you see what is causing the anger, you can more adequately deal with your child's feelings.

Some children may begin to express anger in public situations. They may do this to gain attention, or even sympathy. While encouraging expression of feelings, enforce responsible action (for example controlling anger so that it's expressed privately and not used to manipulate a situation). Parents should not allow themselves to be put in a corner by acting out of fear that their child will get angry.

4. *Ask your children to be open to the person you are dating.* They may not be open to this person just because they do not want *anyone* to be dating their parent. Ask them to be open to see this person as the Lord sees him. They may actually dislike a specific person. Listen to their reasons; they may have some insight you have missed. But ask them to try to be accepting rather than judgmental.

5. *Talk openly about fears that they might have.* Perhaps they are afraid that if you get serious, they will have to move. They may feel their relationship with their other parent will be jeopardized. Talk about these issues, even if you don't have full answers at the moment.

6. *When you date someone for the first time, meet for coffee away from your home.* Then, if you have no interest in seeing this person again, your children will have been spared the process of having to meet and evaluate someone new. It gives you the added advantage of meeting at a neutral location, with your own means of transportation, and for a brief time.

7. *Behave the way you would want your children to behave.* Your kids are watching you closely. They will see if you mean what you teach. They may model you. So be a good example.

What not to do

1. *Don't be so absorbed in your new relationship that your children feel neglected.* Continue to consider their activities and to be the parent you are called to be.

2. *Don't rush this new relationship, and don't rush your children in their acceptance of this person.* Give God time to work in their hearts.

3. *Don't tear down your ex-spouse to build up a new relationship.* No matter how rotten the other parent might seem, he or she is still the parent of your children. You will only make your children feel caught in the middle if you criticize your ex-spouse.

Parents of younger children

Younger children may feel very threatened by the attention paid to their parent by a new person. This can result in the child exhibiting an unusually demanding attitude.

On the other hand, young children may become attached quickly to the new person and strive for inordinate attention.

What to do

1. *Reassure the threatened children that their position with you is secure.* Allow plenty of time alone with them to reinforce that security.

2. *Give the added security of behavioral guidelines.* Sometimes little children are allowed to get away with more after a divorce or a death. There is a certain amount of time when this is healthy. Soon, however, the boundaries must be reestablished. Although your children may resist at first, the added boundaries will produce heightened security.

3. *Allow for expression of feelings in appropriate ways.* As with teens, encourage young children to express their fears and opinions. Allow them to be angry, but not to display anger publicly in the form of tantrums.

What not to do

1. *Don't allow manipulation.* For instance, you bribe a child to go to bed with a treat he would not usually have. So, he demands it again. And you give in.

2. *Don't allow a new person to discipline your children.* You may discuss your children with the new person you are dating and agree with his opinion of discipline. But, you should be the one to administer the discipline.

3. *Don't allow your children to behave badly to get attention.* Handle bad behavior as you would in any other situation. Explain the behavior that is expected, as well as the consequences that will take place if that behavior is not followed. Then be sure to follow through with those consequences when bad behavior occurs—or else you will be challenged on the same behavior again.

Your example to them

If you are a dating single parent, you have a unique opportunity to model behavior before your children that the married parent does not have. And that modeling of behavior goes back to your relationship with the Lord.

Let your children see that the Lord is the focus of your life. Just as you can date, marry, stay single, and still have the Lord come first—they can, too. They can learn that their self-worth is not based on whether they date or who they date. Moreover, they can see a godly, moral relationship lived out in front of them despite all the immorality they see in the world around them.

When not to date

After a divorce or the death of a spouse, there is tremendous pain for the single parent. It is quite normal to be eager to relieve some of that pain with a new relationship.

We are often encouraged to get out and start to "have a life of your own." I have personally been told over and over again not to focus my whole attention on my girls.

Perhaps some people perceive that I do focus too much attention on my girls, but it has been intentional. I have seen a number of other children spend countless nights at home alone while a parent dates. Others have had to quickly adjust to a new stepparent when they have not adequately dealt with the loss or separation of their own parent.

A single parent may feel that he or she has been cheated by having full responsibility for the children. That may be true. But how that responsibility is handled dramatically affects the growth of the children. As parents, we may have to do some things that seem unfair to us for the benefit of our children.

I know of no better investment of time for the single parent than in a close relationship with his or her children. We are only beginning to see the damage that has been done as a result of divorce. Children who are victims of divorce need special love and concern as they grow toward becoming responsible adults. If they feel that the single parent is more concerned with his or her own dating situation than with the child, they may never be able to adequately relate to others.

We have an unhealthy focus on children when we start to live our lives through them. We experience this when we have difficulty letting them go when they are older, or when we pressure them to perform in certain ways to make us happy. We have a healthy focus when we take on that added responsibility we may have been unfairly dealt and lovingly walk with our children through a difficult time.

If we have trouble facing the pain of divorce or death, think of the pain children must face. Putting their needs before our own while we are in the middle of tremendous pain requires sacrificial love. The rewards of that kind of love are immeasurable. What a privilege to be used of the Lord to contribute to the healthy development of our children, even in the rubble of a devastating situation.

Sometimes we can give our children all they need from us and also date. Sometimes we cannot. We only have so much time and energy. If our children are suffering because we are not around or are too tired to help them, then we need to evaluate whether our dating is good for the moment. There may be times in the lives of our children when they need more from us than at other times. We need to be honest about that need and adjust our time accordingly. This does not mean that it is right or wrong to date. It simply means that there may be times when we need to exert our energies in the direction of our children first.

PART VII

Maintaining Godly Relationships

Christian counselor after conversation with woman in same congregation: "A woman came to speak to me to tell me that she had a strong attraction for me that she knew she should not have. My first response was, 'What have I done to make her feel like that?' My second response was an 'ego' response, which made me more interested in why she felt as she did. This could have set up the wrong set of dynamics for an ongoing relationship. Her expressing of her feelings to me created a difficulty for me to work through. In looking back, it created more of a problem for both of us than if she had not ever expressed it."

Christian businessman close to his pastor: "My pastor told me that a woman in the congregation had come to him and admitted to having fantasies about him. He, in turn, told his wife. The result was that his wife developed neurotic behavior that damaged and undermined their ministry in the church. It would have been better had he not communicated that statement to his wife."

TWENTY-ONE

How to Keep from Falling into Immorality

I don't want to make a long list of dos and don'ts, but there are some guidelines we should follow if we want to live godly lives and stay off the pathway to immorality.

Provocative questions

A few years ago I was at a convention attended by many Christians from around the world. It reminded me of the many wonderful times my husband and I had had at such conventions in the past. The atmosphere was upbeat and fun.

Many of the men were there without their wives. I was finding it increasingly difficult to deal with my feelings of loneliness and wondered how some of the men who spent weeks away from home handled this problem in a godly fashion.

I saw an old and trusted married friend sitting in the lobby one afternoon and asked him to join me for a cup of coffee. He did and we talked of his ministry and mine. We discussed the fact that he had been away from home for five weeks and that I had been widowed for several years. With no hidden agenda in mind, I asked him how he handled loneliness. Because it was time for the evening meeting, he suggested we meet afterwards to talk. I agreed, with only a slight feeling of uneasiness.

After the evening session, we met in the lobby, and he abruptly led us out of our hotel. He hailed a cab, and we left for another spot to get a cup of coffee. A red flag was waving in the back of my mind, but I kept ignoring it. Part of my reasoning was because this was a trusted friend and Christian leader, and another part of it was because it felt so good to be out after 9 p.m. with a man!

I loved this brother dearly, but was not physically or emotionally attracted to him. We went to a nearby cafe and, in the course of the next twenty minutes, it became obvious to me that he had more in mind than talking. He immediately backed away when he saw that I was shocked and had no intention of doing anything but talk. We went right back to our hotel, and he politely left me in the lobby by the elevator.

When I got to my room, I was filled with mixed emotions. There was disbelief, excitement, confusion, disgust, and a wonder about what might have happened if I had pursued his suggestion.

Why did this happen? I asked myself that question over and over. What had I done to give the impression that I wanted something "physical"? At first, I couldn't think of anything.

Then I remembered that *I* had initiated the invitation to have coffee and that *I* had asked the question about loneliness. I had not considered his state of mind at that time. He was alone, and had been so for weeks. We were good friends, and he didn't know if I was attracted to him or not.

Of course, my feelings, one way or the other, did not make his approach right, but *I* was the one who started the ball rolling with my provocative question. Having coffee with him in the afternoon in our hotel coffee shop wasn't wrong. Asking him a pressing question wasn't wrong. Having coffee with him late at night away from the convention was very risky, and continuing the discussion about the provocative question was wrong and unfair.

Don't listen to complaints about the spouse.

Another situation that can lead to unhealthy involvement is to listen to a man complain about his wife. The one who listens to this kind of complaint can be a single or a married woman. The office often seems to be the most conducive spot for this kind of conversation. Women in the working world need to have their antennae up all the time. After all, they spend about twice as much time with a man as his wife does—and relate to him on a subject very dear to him: his work.

It is tempting to be a good listener and to encourage a man you respect. What happens, however, when we hear the woes of a dissatisfied husband? We may not say it, but we automatically think, "I could make this man happy." Pretty soon we start thinking about actually making him happy, and, depending on the situation, one thing can lead to another. If you know a man who is already expressing a need for "another" woman, be careful you don't start to meet that need.

If a man complains to me about his wife, I suggest that he talk to another man. (I refer him to someone who is either a committed Christian experienced to help in these matters or to a professional counselor.) Then I change the subject. This sounds a little cold, but it closes the door on a potentially explosive situation.

Don't fish for compliments.

Maybe you are married to a man who does not pay you very many compliments. So you go fishing. You try to solicit compliments from other men. This can lead to getting not only the compliments, but something else that you didn't bargain for.

Perhaps you are single and have a poor self-image. It is dangerous to tease men just enough to see if you are desirable to them.

Why did Esau sell his birthright? Genesis 25:29-32 gives us the answer:

> Once when Jacob was cooking some stew, Esau came in from the open country, famished. He said to Jacob, "Quick, let me have some of that red stew! I'm famished!"
>
> Jacob replied, "First sell me your birthright."
>
> "Look, I am about to die," Esau said. "What good is the birthright to me?"

He sold the privilege of his birthright because he was famished! The Christian world is filled with love-famished people. When I was in a loving marriage relationship, I could not understand what drove believers to immorality. Now that I have spent years alone, I better understand what it means to be famished.

What we must recognize is that selling our birthright for mere stew is not the answer. Proverbs 27:7 says, "He who is full loathes honey, but to the hungry even what is bitter tastes sweet." It is a lie to believe that our needs for intimate love that are met temporarily by someone else's husband or wife can satisfy our deep inner longings and will somehow go unpunished.

If you sense "electricity"

Married women tend to be a little apprehensive when a single woman comes around—and, unfortunately, for good reason.

If I'm talking to a married man and sense a little electricity in the air between him and me, I direct my attention to his wife, and even take a physical step back from him. Then, when I see this couple again, they both seem friendly and at ease with me. It gives me a fulfilling sense of reward for taking a very small, almost unnoticed incident, and saying without words that I am not emotionally interested in this woman's husband. I can have better quality friendships with men when I have the additional friendship of their wives.

The prolonged stare

In normal conversation you meet the eyes of the other person for a certain amount of time, then one or the other glances away. This is the way of conversation. But when a special feeling is developing for the other person, this is signaled by the prolonged stare. This could be a signal telling the other person that he or she is special, and a promise of more to come.

If you have a special feeling for another person—and it does happen even with godly, married men and women—subdue it. Don't signal it to that other person. If you keep it to yourself and ask the Lord to help you deal with it, then you are the only one involved. But as soon as you signal to the other person, then *he* (or she) is involved. This ignites a fire in many people.

The lingering touch

The physical touch, even more than the stare, is a definite giveaway. It is when you shake hands with another person and hold hands for just a second too long. Everyone knows the social custom of how long to touch in this way. When that touch lingers, it is a definite signal.

If a man comes by your desk and puts his hand on your arm or shoulder just a little bit too long, he is telling you something. You are telling him something if you do it to him.

Don't let the touch linger.

Letting the other person know

It is bad enough to signal your feelings to a married person with an extended look or touch, but to tell that person outright is putting gasoline on a fire.

The normal tendency when feelings begin to grow strong for another person is to tell him. In the Christian world, we spiritualize this mistake by asking the person to pray for us. After all, we are taught to be open and vulnerable with other believers.

But imagine what happens in a man's mind when a Christian woman says to him, "I want you to pray for me in one particular area. I am struggling with my feelings toward you." I have shared this illustration with some of my trusted married men friends, and they all agreed that knowing that a woman is attracted to them lights a fire in them.

Instead of being able to pray in a godly fashion, they now have a struggle of their own. Their ego has been ignited and a desire to feed that fire competes with the desire to be godly. It is far better never to mention how you feel.

When you tell your feelings to someone who is unavailable to you, you are taking a step in the process toward total involvement. Discussion follows about how the feelings began, there is a fishing for compliments, there is response to the compliments, praying together, determining to be godly about it all, mentally repeating what has been shared, the desire to discuss it again, more discussion, a little touch, more prayer, determination to keep things right, mentally replaying the little touch, talking about it again, another touch—and deeper and deeper into the trap of emotional dependency that leads to immorality.

It is more difficult for another person to change his behavior patterns after you tell him about your feelings. He may not even feel the need for a change. I have seen many situations with this kind of relationship between a married man and a single woman. The woman has a much higher frustration level than the man. She goes home alone; he goes home to a wife and family. Many men feel that the friendship with the single woman is a "blessing" for her and does no harm to him or his marriage. He has an appropriate outlet for his sexual desires at home, and has the ego boost of the interest of another woman besides his wife. Because nothing "sexual" is going on with the single woman (or so he tells himself), he feels their friendship is okay before the Lord.

The woman, on the other hand, becomes a kind of spiritual mistress. She is not a mistress in a consummated physical affair, but she meets ego needs for him at the expense of her own well-being. A woman in this kind of situation is constantly frustrated. She is settling for far worse than second best. There is no way to win. Because of her commitment to Christ, she does not move to break up a marriage. But because of her unwillingness, or unawareness, to call this dependency a sin, she is trapped in an unfulfilling, ungodly predicament.

And remember that some men, even if they don't have the depth of feelings for you that you have for them, will take advantage of your emotional state to get some "free sex."

Make it a firm rule never to tell a married person about your feelings about him or her.

Understand the way your spouse is perceived

I have heard many married women who are at home describe their husbands in the dullest of terms. "Oh, no one would ever be interested in him," they express with incredible naiveté. Because such a woman is not out in the business world on a daily basis, she does not see the way her husband is perceived. He may be a slob around the house, but the model of attractiveness in the office. How often have we seen marriages break up because the wife did not "appreciate" the husband?

Most of us, men and women, are two "images"; the one at home and the one out in public. And a degree of that is okay. The problem is that when one party in the marriage is totally unaware of the image of the other, there is room for vulnerability.

A man who feels unappreciated at home may well respond to feeling appreciated out of the home. Just being aware that the guy whose underwear you wash may be a hunk in disguise is a start.

It is really a matter of taking for granted what we are accustomed to. The longer we live with someone, the more we may miss the uniqueness of that person. There is a popular song that says, "Don't look at your man in the same old way." Give a little extra care, a compliment, a sign of appreciation.

I can almost hear, "But you don't live with him!"

Exactly right. And, neither do the women he works with. Everyone but a man's wife (or a woman's husband) perceives him without the flaws that intimacy reveals. It is not a matter of forgetting the flaws and blindly accepting any behavior. It is simply to realize that this person you live with is someone others may find very tempting. If you want to stay in a faithful relationship with him or her, be sure that needs for acceptance are being met by you, not just others.

The gray areas of behavior

There are some areas that may not be technically wrong, but are borderline. These gray areas often make it especially difficult to be really honest.

The key in evaluating our behavior here is to look at the motives. Ungodly actions can be somewhat easily detected because they can be seen, but we can more easily fool others and ourselves with ungodly motives. After all, no one really knows our thoughts except ourselves and God.

What guidelines can you follow to know if your behavior is consistent with a godly walk?

1. *Analyze your relationships.* First, take a look at all of your relationships. Is there anyone of the opposite sex who is unavailable (because of marriage or some other reason), yet who arouses feelings of flirtation, romance, and excitement within you? Since you are asking this privately of yourself, you can be absolutely honest. Without honesty, there is no way out of inappropriate behavior.

2. *Change your behavioral patterns.* When you admit to yourself that you *are* attracted to someone who is unavailable, you must change your behavior immediately. The degree of dependency you have on the other person will, to a large degree, determine the degree of change needed. You may need to simply stop seeing each other altogether, or perhaps go so far as to leave your job. If you are already emotionally involved, remember that this kind of involvement is an actual step in the process that leads to immorality.

If the other person knows about your feelings for him, tell him that you realize the relationship is wrong and that you are going to change your part of it. Inform him that you will no longer have personal or intimate conversations, that you will relate to him only in a business way (if you work with him) or only in a detached way socially (if you know him only socially).

It is important to resist trying to convert this person to your point of view. Just tell—and go. We are releasing him back to the Lord. You will minister to this person by getting out of his life. Chapter 22 deals with a new perspective of loving and encouraging others. This perspective enables us to help the people we love in a truly unselfish way.

Make sure you are aware of your own dangerous behavioral patterns. If most of your decisions are based on this other person's opinions and you find yourself starting to call him for advice, call someone else instead. If you make up reasons to work late to be around this person, then start going home on time. Stop discussing personal issues. Stop feeding the need to have this other person's approval on all your actions.

If he begins to question your change in behavior, answer as briefly as possible in a matter-of-fact way. For instance, if asked why you are leaving the office on time instead of working late, tell him you have decided to have a more balanced life and to spend time on things other than work. He may question this, but that's all right, because it's true. Chances are that he already suspects that you like being around him, and he may like the attention, too. But don't give in to the temptation to tell him about the attraction. That will only lead to trouble.

Once, at a banquet, I was talking to a married Christian executive who had a single secretary. We began talking about the subject of this book. He asked me questions about office relationships. After talking in general terms, he admitted that he was concerned that his secretary might have stronger feelings for him than were appropriate. We discussed how he could break her dependency on him. He said that his trying to be an encouragement to her and helping her in areas of her life outside the office may have fed the dependency.

It is fine to want to help others, but if they are relying on us to an unhealthy extent, it may be necessary to back off. A few weeks after the banquet, I received a note from this man thanking me for our discussion. He had returned to the office and changed some of his behavior. He felt that he and his secretary now had a less dependent, much more healthy relationship. His new behavior even resulted in her reaching out in other directions and developing new relationships to help meet her needs for friendship.

If that change can occur without forcing physical distance between two people, that is good. But if it cannot, then one party may need to move away from the other.

If one person in the relationship does not see the need for a change, then a tremendous amount of pressure is put on the person who knows that change is necessary. The ability to hold fast under pressure will determine the success of righting the relationship.

The most challenging difficulty is being able to see the sin involved even when there is an absence of physical contact. Emotional dependency is an elusive culprit. Its crippling effect on a person may go unnoticed for years.

Part of the sin is letting emotions control actions. The other part of the sin is that of covetousness. It is impossible to serve two masters. Any time that something or someone other than the Lord has control of what we do, we are in trouble. If we're to be absolutely honest, we would have to admit that situations like this occur because we *want* to be with someone we don't have the right to be with. All the women I have talked to who are personally in this kind of situation have, at one time or another, wished they were married to the men involved.

Is it okay to have lunch with a married man? How do you feel about him? Is there a truly legitimate reason to have lunch with him? If the reasons are legitimate but the feelings are inappropriate, then find another person to meet the legitimate reasons. If you need to meet with your accountant for a necessary reason but you know that you have a growing attraction for him, find a new accountant. Or, change your thoughts and behavior to the degree that you have the correct motives before God for being with the accountant.

What to do

Dr. Howard Hendricks of Dallas Theological Seminary spoke one evening on the topic of "The Secret to Godly Living." As he began his message, everyone sat anxiously with pen in hand. I will never forget the initial letdown when he began by telling the group that he had nothing new to say; that we had all heard it before. Read the Word, pray, fellowship. What more can be said? The thing now is to *do* them!

The last thing we feel like doing when we are depressed or in the middle of a negative thought pattern is to read the Bible. After all, we know what it says. Reading wouldn't probably make us feel any better at all. So why try? We try because the Christian life is one of *obedience,* not feelings. What we do out of obedience, God rewards in love. The rewards are not always felt instantly, but they will come.

Our choice is this: to do what He says even though we feel terrible, or to not do what He says and feel awful anyway. Doing what He says, over time, gives strength to fight the battle better. We may still be in the same war, but we will be advancing against the enemy. Defeat comes only when we give up.

In order to determine proper behavior for a given situation, we have to "examine our ways and test them, and . . . return to the Lord" (Lamentations 3:40). Ungodly behavior can often be traced to an attempt to meet a felt need. Some women use relationships with married men to satisfy needs formerly met for them by their husbands. In my situation at the convention, I was looking for an answer to my felt need of loneliness, and my friend was looking for the answer to the same thing. (I wanted words; he wanted physical contact.)

The first step in correcting our behavior in "gray areas" is to identify unmet needs in your own life. After doing this, you need to discover how you are trying to meet those needs. Are you trying to meet them in a godly manner, or are you trying according to the world's way?

TWENTY-TWO

Love: The World's View Versus the Biblical View

Alex and Melanie had been having an adulterous affair for about four months. Alex was divorced and Melanie was married to an unbeliever. They met at church and became friends as a result of time spent in a Sunday school class. The relationship began innocently enough, but, after progressing through the stages described earlier in this book, they found themselves ensnared in adultery.

Their affair remained undiscovered, but Alex experienced a growing sense of guilt. He had only been a believer for a few years, but had successfully changed his lifestyle to become a committed Christian walking with the Lord. His affair with Melanie insidiously caught him unawares. Lack of control was evident before he even realized that control was needed.

Alex's convictions that this relationship was ungodly led him to seek the advice of one of the Christian counselors who attended the same church. The counselor was unsurprised by the all-too-common situation, but did have a concerned and caring attitude. He listened patiently, then gave advice that seemed harsh and unnecessary to Alex.

The counselor recommended one conversation with Melanie to end the relationship, then—no further contact. He recommended that Alex change Sunday school classes and simply refuse any contact at all. Alex's concern was that Melanie would not understand and would be terribly hurt. The counselor agreed that she probably would have a rough time, but that a clean and total break would be less painful than a slow, agonizing one. Besides, Alex and Melanie would probably not have the strength to stay away from each other if they remained in touch.

Alex was still not convinced that this drastic a measure was necessary, but he agreed to do it. That night after a church function that Alex and Melanie both attended, he told her of his decision. Her response was hurt, anger, and confusion. Alex felt awful. He felt as if he were kicking someone he loved. The counselor's words were fresh in his mind, so he followed through and ended the relationship.

During the next few weeks, Alex saw Melanie only fleetingly around church. He wanted to explain, but resisted the temptation to start a conversation. He talked to his counselor several more times, and the counselor continued to encourage him to hold fast to his decision. He also cautioned Alex to be prepared for a phone call from Melanie when he least expected it. Alex doubted this would happen, but did agree to hang up the phone if she called.

The call came. Alex said he couldn't talk and hung up. He was angry. He was angry at the counselor and angry at himself for hurting another believer whom he had wronged. The next Sunday in church, Alex saw Melanie before the church service. They exchanged polite hellos. Their eyes lingered, and Alex felt a rush of emotion. Melanie looked so hurt and confused. He tarried just a moment and told her how good she looked. That was all: a brief moment, one remark meant to ease some pain and encourage a friend.

That night Melanie called Alex. She began by saying that she only wanted to ask him one question. He started to hang up, but didn't. What was the harm in answering one question? And besides, he had hurt her enough. They talked for about ten minutes. Alex felt apprehension creeping back into his thinking. He ended the conversation in a pleasant, but definite way. He told her that, perhaps, sometime in the future they could meet for lunch and get caught up on each other's lives, but not now.

Alex told himself he felt okay about the encounter in church and the phone call. He spoke to his counselor friend a few days later and told him what had happened. Alex's tone was aggressive and defensive. He knew what the counselor would say. It had been a step backward. What Alex had meant to be an encouragement to Melanie was really harmful to her. Alex still didn't understand completely, but agreed to try again not to contact her.

Melanie did call again. Alex hung up. She called one more time. He hung up. Then the calls stopped. Alex felt responsible for unnecessarily hurting a friend. But he stayed away from her. He didn't return to the same Sunday school class. He spoke politely when they met, but avoided looking directly into her eyes. It hurt him terribly. He didn't like himself and he was uncomfortable with his actions. He followed through because he earnestly wanted to get his walk with the Lord straight. He knew that even though this approach seemed harsh, it was better than the adulterous relationship had been.

Alex began to focus on his own walk with God and less on what was happening with Melanie. He seemed stronger in his control of his thoughts and actions. The Lord brought changes and new opportunities into his life that redirected his thinking from Melanie and from the lifestyle that relationship represented. When she did come to mind, Alex felt regret and pain over what had happened, but released her to the Lord and accepted the fact that she was out of his life.

Because of a job change, Alex moved to another city. As he was going through the process of saying goodbye to old friends, he thought of calling Melanie. Because of an inner hesitation, he didn't call her. During the following year, he had occasion to return to town and visit his old church. As he drove into the parking lot, an emotional rush come over him. He thought of Melanie and felt an old familiar pain. But it lasted only a moment.

As Alex walked into the church, he found himself face-to-face with Melanie. She looked lovelier than he had ever seen her. She was surprised to see him, but merely smiled warmly as they shook hands. They spoke a few minutes about their current lives. Melanie had become more active in church, and she and her husband were now in counseling. She had a calm confidence that Alex had never seen in her. He told her of his new job and of his growing relationship with the Lord. Neither of them mentioned the past. It would have been so out of place now that they had both grown. Another friend came over, and the conversation with Melanie ended.

As Alex sat in church, he thought about their meeting. He gratefully felt no guilt, no regret, no desire for the old relationship to be alive again. He knew also, without her having said so, that Melanie felt the same way.

The world's view of love

The Bible tells us to be loving and encouraging to one another—to carry one another's burdens. Our worldly society has so twisted these words that we have to step way back from our own actions to see if we really are loving and encouraging to others.

In the relationship just described, the loving approach would *appear* to be to change the relationship gradually, to make a transition from lovers to friends, to take sex out but keep love in.

The reason Alex felt he was hurting Melanie so much was because that was what the world would have him believe. How could it be wrong to tell a woman she really looks good when she really does look good? How could encouraging someone over the telephone be so wrong? Isn't it right to help meet someone's need for concern and caring when we feel we can do so?

The biblical view of love

The reason these actions of the world are wrong is because they do not ultimately accomplish what needs to be accomplished. Melanie had needs met by a man whom God did not intend to meet her needs. If Alex and Melanie had maintained a strictly platonic yet godly friendship, there would have been ways he could have encouraged her. We do that all the time with each other, as long as the relationship is one God approves of.

But when we cross over the line of proper, biblical relationships, we forfeit the right to be used of God in a positive way in the other person's life. We'll only be used in an ungodly way. The encouragement Melanie needed had to be strong enough to stop even seeing Alex. Any compliment from him only encouraged her in exactly the opposite direction. A compliment from Alex was not like a compliment from anyone else. It allowed her to hang on to a hope that he was still attracted to her.

What Alex saw as a painful kick directed at a friend was really the most loving and encouraging thing he could do. As he continued to refuse to let Melanie have her needs met by him, he stepped out of the way and allowed God to move in and redirect Melanie's dependence.

It is a painful experience to be misunderstood by someone we care about. To be willing to suffer for the good of another is the highest form of true love. It is the kind of love Christ suffered for us. If we want to be authentic burden bearers, we must carry the burdens all the way to the Cross. There we lay down the loved one and the responsibility for his or her happiness, and we walk away. We cannot do for that person what only Christ can do.

Real burden bearing is when we are willing to be thought of as cold and uncaring, to be misunderstood, and to be hurt ourselves for attempting to be godly.

Our view of love must become one of tough love. It is tough to change ungodly patterns. It is tough to watch people suffer. It is also tough to hurt and to see hurt inflicted because of our disobedient actions. But it often requires tough love to lead people back toward the Lord.

Maintaining godly relationships

When we understand that true love does not mean we have to meet all the needs others have, we are free to act biblically toward them. We learn not to allow others to have inordinate dependency on us.

By continually pointing people back to Christ and a lifestyle of walking with Him, we enhance their ability to grow as Christians. This doesn't in any way mean we become so independent that we don't need other people in our lives. It does mean that we understand that obedience to Christ allows for proper interdependence with others.

God never wants you to be disobedient to Him as you serve others' needs. No matter how great a need may be, if there is no godly answer, we have to wait in godly obedience instead of taking an ungodly detour.

Again, maintaining godly relationships is accomplished by making our relationship with Christ the first priority of our lives and by choosing to obey God. This may mean choosing obedience over what appears to be helping others, over relieving their temporary pain, over what appears to be good results.

Once we are aware of the process that leads to immorality, we need to constantly check ourselves. If the slightest red flag of danger pops up, we must honestly evaluate motives and choose obedience instead of compromise. As soon as we give in to compromise, we are weakening our ability to stay on the path with Jesus Christ.

TWENTY-THREE

The Eternal Perspective

"Then I saw a new heaven and a new earth, for the first heaven and the first earth had passed away. . . . And I heard a loud voice from the throne saying, 'Now the dwelling of God is with men, and he will live with them. They will be his people, and God himself will be with them and be their God. He will wipe every tear from their eyes. There will be no more death or mourning or crying or pain, for the old order of things has passed away.' He who was seated on the throne said, 'I am making everything new!'" (Revelation 21:1-5).

Though one of our deepest longings would be to live without any pain, we can't even dream of what that would be like because our consciousness can't even imagine it. This description of total happiness from the book of Revelation gives us an idea of the spectacular reward for those disciples who persevere through the trials of life on this earth.

The reality of heaven

There was a moment on that day when my husband was killed in a fiery hot-air balloon crash that profoundly substantiated my belief in heaven. Most people have not experienced such a graphic event to make heaven seem so real.

But if we believe in Christ and have accepted Him as our Savior, then we can all accept the reality of heaven as utterly true. We can trust Him for heaven because it is an essential part of our salvation.

I recently heard of a professing Christian who claimed not to believe in heaven. Although I have not met this person, I find it very difficult to understand how or even why someone would want to be a Christian and not believe in heaven. Heaven is the reward for trusting in Christ, culminating a lifetime of living for Him. It is the sure hope of something better than we have now.

If we can claim just the opening verses at the beginning of this chapter, we need no further description of heaven. A place that has no more crying or pain would be enough to hold on to in difficult times.

Living between hope and contentment

Being consistent in walking with Christ means learning to live between Jeremiah 29:11 and Philippians 4:11-13.

> "I know the plans I have for you," declares the LORD, "plans to prosper you and not to harm you, plans to give you hope and a future." (Jeremiah 29:11)

> I have learned to be content whatever the circumstances. I know what it is to be in need, and I know what it is to have plenty. I have learned the secret of being content in any and every situation, whether well fed or hungry, whether living in plenty or in want. I can do everything through him who gives me strength. (Philippians 4:11-13)

If God could and would do anything at all for you, what would you want Him to do? If you are having an immoral relationship, maybe you want Him to somehow make that right. Perhaps you want Him to restore your marriage. Or bring a love into your life to relieve the pain of being alone.

How do we live if God chooses not to answer that request? If we have a request that is in line with a godly walk and we desire it desperately, what do we do if it does not come about?

Somehow we must learn to live between the hope that He will accomplish what we long for and a true sense of contentment if He does not. God promises that He has a perfect plan for us. But as He says in Jeremiah, *He* is the one who knows the plan, not us.

As we seek to walk with Him, we can hope and pray for a godly plan and move in that direction. The important thing is that we take no ungodly actions to achieve that goal, thinking that the door will still be open despite our disobedience. If we start out pursuing a path that we feel is godly but we find that continuing along that path means committing an ungodly action, it will no longer be God's plan for us. More accurately, it is not God's plan for the end *we* initially had in mind.

If, for example, you are asking God to bring someone into your life to marry, and then romance with a certain person enters the picture, you may move forward as this possibly being the will of God. But if, along the way, something ungodly enters the relationship, then you should strongly consider that it is probably not God's will for you to marry this person. It may have been God's will for you to learn something from the experience, but it is certainly not the godly plan you originally saw.

This should not destroy your hope of meeting someone else who is God's choice for you. You shouldn't take a totally negative view when a particular situation doesn't work out for you. Instead, you can learn from one experience and still have your hope for the future intact.

In Philippians 4:11-13, Paul is stating that he has "learned the secret of being content." The two key words here are *learned* and *secret.* We often think we can read a book or attend a seminar and come away knowing how to be content. "Learned" implies that it is a process and that it is not natural. "Secret" means that it is not easily seen. Paul's answer is that we can do all things through Christ. Again, ***it all goes back to the relationship with the Lord.*** Learning the secret of contentment means learning who Christ is and what that means to us individually.

In living a godly life, we are constantly living with hope for the future and learning contentment for where we are now. The important ingredient in this walk is to continually choose godly ways to keep that hope alive and the contentment a reality.

A pure walk

The entrance fee into heaven has been paid for us by Christ's death on the Cross. Heaven is a free gift. It is gained by nothing of our own efforts and all of Christ's. Why, then, do we even have to live a godly life? Why not go ahead and have an affair?

We live a godly life for two reasons. The first is out of gratitude. Christ says, "If you love me, you will obey what I command" (John 14:15). He does not tell us that we enter a relationship with Him based on our ability to keep His commandments. But He does tell us that if we love Him, we will keep His commandments. We learn to truly love Jesus as we become aware of the enormity of what He did for us.

That is one of the reasons why it is important to have a belief in heaven. The price He paid purchased a place in heaven for us. We need to believe this spiritual fact in order to be grateful for it. If someone saved our life here on earth, we would undoubtedly feel gratitude. If we realize that Christ did, in fact, save our lives, then we will be better able to live out of a heart of love.

The second reason we live a godly life is that we are to be like Christ. We cannot be perfect, but we are to strive to emulate Him in all we do. Also, if we belong to Him and do not live a godly life, we will pay for those sins. We will have heaven, but we will also suffer for our ungodliness. This may not always seem fair to us, but it is the way God has established things.

Obedience is a byproduct of faith. Personal fulfillment and longings met in a godly way are byproducts of obedience.

Quality of life

There is a certain quality of life that results from a godly walk with the Lord. You seldom hear about it because few attain the level of relationship with the Lord that results in genuine communion with Him.

I have had only a *few* moments on a level rising far above my circumstances, but at least I have had those few. I have known great saints who have experienced *many* such moments but many more believers who have not yet been with the Lord on a truly intimate level.

Charles Haddon Spurgeon described this kind of communion in his commentary on Psalm 91:

> The blessings here promised are not for all believers, but for those who live in close fellowship with God. . . . Those who through rich grace obtain unusual and continuous communion

> with God, so as to abide in Christ and Christ in them, become possessors of rare and special benefits, which are missed by those who follow afar off and grieve the Holy Spirit of God. . . . When the heart is enamoured of the Lord, all taken up with Him, and intensely attached to Him, the Lord will recognize the sacred flame, and preserve the man who bears it in his bosom. It is love—love set upon God, which is the distinguishing mark of those whom the Lord secures from ill. . . . The man described in this Psalm fills out the measure of his days, and whether he dies young or old, he is quite satisfied with life, and is content to leave it. He shall rise from life's banquet as a man who has had enough, and would not have more even if he could.[15]

How do we become recipients of such rich grace? I do not know the full answer. But I do know that obedience motivated by love is the beginning. It requires a willingness to settle for obedience instead of merely seeking relief from pain. It is a willingness to live a life marked by honor, and to see glory in heaven and not here on earth. The results of this kind of dedicated life are forever.

There is a plaque that reads, "Life is the childhood of our immortality." If we could just grasp that truth, we would be so much more willing to let go of our own selfish desires here in exchange for a life of perfection in heaven.

Longings fulfilled

The deepest longing of my heart right now is to feel loved. I have experienced being loved in the past—both by God and by people. Right this minute, sitting at my typewriter, I am not *feeling* deeply loved. I realize that part of my longing is directed toward a very human man. I also realize that even if I marry that man, he will not ultimately be able to meet my deep longing. He can bring joy and limited fulfillment. He can give me happy moments. But he is not the answer to my longings. Even if he were the most perfect man alive, he would fall short of the ability to love me perfectly.

There is only one answer to the longing that I feel right this moment. The answer is the awareness I experience of my secure relationship with Jesus Christ. The relationship is there, but the feeling of the fulfillment of my longings will come only when I am aware of that perfect love and acceptance from my Savior.

Heaven

"I did not see a temple in the city, because the Lord God Almighty and the Lamb are its temple. The city does not need the sun or the moon to shine on it, for the glory of God gives it light, and the Lamb is its lamp. The nations will walk by its light, and the kings of the earth will bring their splendor into it. On no day will its gates ever be shut, for there will be no night there. The glory and honor of the nations will be brought into it. Nothing impure will ever enter it, nor will anyone who does what is shameful or deceitful, but only those whose names are written in the Lamb's book of life. . . . The throne of God and of the Lamb will be in the city, and his servants will serve him. They will see his face, and his name will be on their foreheads" (Revelation 21:22-27, 22:3-4).

I know that I will be in heaven—not because of anything in me, but because of Christ. He has forgiven me. He has bought me. He continues to entreat me to walk with Him. He gives me the power to walk that walk. He will someday enable me to say with Paul that I have fought the good fight, finished the race, kept the faith. He will greet me at the gate of heaven and say, "Well done, thou good and faithful servant."

He will look deeply into my soul, and then I will completely experience the fulfillment of my deepest longing. That fulfillment will be forever and will be incomparable to anything experienced before. What I will see then, I see dimly and fleetingly now, but I am unable to continually grasp it.

I will see His look. I will recognize it for what it is. It will be all I need forever.

He will look at me with perfect love.

PART VIII

Restoration: Picking Up the Pieces

Christian man after involvement with coworker: "The biggest thing is guilt. The guilt drives your self-esteem so much lower. I didn't feel worthy of being restored. That's a helpless feeling. I had the feeling that God really couldn't forgive this *one. It makes it hard to seek restoration.*

"I am really grateful that my wife stood by me in the process of restoration. If she had not been supportive, I am not sure how I could have handled it. Without her attitude, I believe that the whole relationship would have failed. My wife trusted God, and that strengthened her. And, that, in turn, strengthened me at my weakest link."

Christian woman after husband was involved with another woman: "My self-esteem was destroyed. I found it really easy to compare myself with the woman my husband had been involved with. I had to learn to accept myself as God accepts me."

Christian man after involvement with counselee: "I had no question of forgiveness before God. I knew I would be disciplined, but forgiven. I found it much harder to forgive myself because of the destruction I had brought to myself and to the people who had known and trusted me. I felt my sin invalidated everything I had done positively in the past.

"Restoration is still an ongoing struggle. I have had high expectations for myself and let many people down. I feel like I have been put on a shelf for Christ. It is a frustrating situation."

TWENTY-FOUR

Living with Yourself

The battle royal is over. The adulterous relationship is ended. The immoral relationship between two singles is through.

You are the one who was in the relationship—or you are married to the party involved. There is intense pain and a whirlpool of emotions. Life is so murky. You have inflicted hurt, and you have been hurt.

You are a Christian. You have humiliated the name of Christ and your own name. Or, you are a victim of the humiliation by virtue of your marriage to the offending party. What happens now?

What happens now depends on you. It does not depend on anyone else. No one, that is, but God. It depends on what you do with you, and what God decides to do with you.

David

We have already looked at the account of David and Bathsheba. Let's look at Psalm 51 to see what David did with himself after he was confronted by Nathan.

David stated, "Have mercy on me, O God, according to your unfailing love; according to your great compassion blot out my transgressions. Wash away all my iniquity and cleanse me from my sin" (Psalm 51:1-2).

As you face yourself, now, with the reality of your sin in the open—call out to God. Whether your sin is known by others or just between you and God, it has now been acknowledged. You have turned from it, but now you must face the ramifications of your actions. Call out to God. Ask Him, as David did, to have mercy. Ask Him to cleanse you. It doesn't matter that you don't know exactly how He will do it.

David went on to say, "For I know my transgressions, and my sin is always before me. Against you, you only, have I sinned and done what is evil in your sight" (Psalm 51:3-4).

Recognized sin is not easily forgotten. It is ever in our memory. Even though David knew that God would forgive his sin, he still had the memory of it to deal with. It is important for us to acknowledge that our sin is against God. Sin hurts others deeply, but the primary offense is toward God.

David believed that God was capable of making him clean again. "Cleanse me with hyssop, and I will be clean; wash me, and I will be whiter than snow" (Psalm 51:7). He may not have *felt* clean, but he knew that God considered him such because of God's forgiveness. We have forgiveness because of Christ. We will still experience consequences for our sin, but we have forgiveness through Christ.

David asked God, "Create in me a pure heart, O God, and renew a steadfast spirit within me" (Psalm 51:10). Ask God to change your heart, too. If your heart has been deceived, ask God to make it pure. A steadfast spirit is one that will remain faithful to God in times of turmoil. Ask for that spirit to be restored in you.

David realized the bottom line of what God wanted from him: "The sacrifices of God are a broken spirit; a broken and contrite heart, O God, you will not despise" (Psalm 51:17). If you have been in an immoral relationship and you have now repented, you know what the psalmist meant when he spoke of a broken heart. A broken heart that is the result of sin has a heaviness that is oppressive. In time, that heaviness will lift, and you will feel the joy of the Lord again.

In the meantime, you will be in a process of healing and accepting yourself again. In order to live with yourself, even if you are the victim in the situation, you must learn to look at yourself as God does. But how does God view us?

If you are the offender

If you are a believer and you have been in an immoral relationship, you have the opportunity to be restored because of the redemptive work of Jesus Christ. Even with that vindication, you will experience some inevitable pain.

Shame is a painful emotion brought on by a consciousness of guilt or sin. Acknowledgment of sin results in shame. It is a painful thing for us to realize the pain we cause others as a result of that sin.

In the July 10, 1987 issue of *Christianity Today,* Gordon MacDonald was interviewed after resigning from the presidency of Inter-Varsity Christian Fellowship. Here is a man experiencing the pain of his mistakes. He is conscious of his guilt and feels shame over it.

What should we do with feelings of shame? Dr. MacDonald said in that same article, "We [he and his wife] are going into quiet and we have no plans for the future until God gives us some sense of direction."[16] The passing of time is necessary for healing us from our consciousness of guilt. God can restore, but it takes time. It is useless to try to outrun pain.

Forgiveness and pain are not exclusive. We are told in 1 John 1:9, "If we confess our sins, [God] is faithful and just and will forgive us our sins and purify us from all unrighteousness." We can be forgiven and yet still experience pain.

Constant feelings of guilt over sin that is confessed and completely repented of is not of the Lord. He says that it is forgiven. Satan can completely debilitate a believer, however, by constantly reminding him of past sins.

When you find your thoughts dwelling on the past, focus on the reality of Christ in your life. The situation you are in is the very situation (among a multitude of others) that He went to the Cross for. Philippians 3:10 says, "I want to know Christ and the power of his resurrection and the fellowship of sharing in his sufferings. . . ." Then in verses 12-14, Paul continues, "Not that I have already obtained all this, or have already been made perfect, but I press on to take hold of that for which Christ Jesus took hold of me. Brothers, I do not consider myself yet to have taken hold of it. But one thing I do: Forgetting what is behind and straining toward what is ahead, I press on toward the goal to win the prize for which God has called me heavenward in Christ Jesus."

Take your guilt feelings and lay them aside. They will no doubt surface in your mind again, but just lay them aside again. Rest in quietness before the Lord. Experience the pain of the consequences of your sin, but not the living over again of the sin itself. Look ahead with the confident anticipation that God is still calling you in the direction of heaven.

Begin to see yourself as a believer being transformed by God. In process. Not completed. You have made a mess of things. A serious mess, perhaps. But God is bigger than any mess you may have made. Leave your guilt at the foot of the Cross. He paid for it there. Jesus has handled your guilt. All you have to handle is your next step. Just the next one.

And the next step is—whatever you are responsible for next. Maybe it is to go to work today. Or perhaps you need to rest from your battle. You may need to spend time with your children to help restore their confidence in your presence in the home. Your spouse may need some of your energy in some expression of renewed love.

As you regain your footing in your walk with the Lord, do not be surprised when the old temptations return. In the middle of repentance and remorse, we initially feel that we will *never* be tempted to fall for that particular sin again. But Satan is persistent, and will undoubtedly return.

Being tempted again does not mean that you will fall again. In fact, if you have truly repented and suffered through the restoration process, you may be better prepared for an attack than someone who has never been tempted. Just don't let the temptation catch you by surprise. Flee quickly. Don't even entertain a moment's worth of folly thinking on it. Flee.

In your relationship with your spouse, you may feel a wide range of emotions. If you are in counseling, be open with the counselor about your feelings. Be willing to go the extra mile to restore your damaged relationship. In the next chapter, we look at the role of the husband and wife after their marriage has been touched by adultery.

There is a final part of the process of learning again to live with ourselves that we may feel we do not have the right to experience: grieving our losses.

My mother recently had her leg amputated. She underwent a series of three operations before her condition stabilized. During the uncertainty of these operations, I experienced feelings of uneasiness. After the third operation, she began to heal and was on the road to recovery. My uneasy feelings remained. It wasn't until I correctly identified them that I was able to deal with them.

Ever since my husband was killed, I have had a "sense" deep inside me that is always there. Sometimes it is more evident than others. Sometimes I go for long stretches without experiencing pain because of it. But it is always there and does resurface. I realized when I thought about my mother and the loss of her leg that I was experiencing that same "sense." I felt a personal loss. It was more than a sympathy for my mother's loss. It was a feeling of loss to me as well. Of course, I was concerned about my mother's pain and altered lifestyle. But, as with the death of my husband, there was something in me now that hurt.

I allowed myself to grieve over my mother's loss that was also my own. I did not feel I really had the right to feel loss, but I acknowledged that I did feel it. I went through the stages of grieving and finally accepted that loss.

Often, after an immoral relationship, you may feel that you do not have the right to grieve that loss. Because it was something in your life that should not have been there, you deny that you feel loss at all. It is difficult to heal something that is not acknowledged. If feelings of grief are not brought up and worked out, they can surface later in damaging ways.

Suppose, in the midst of restoration, you feel anger deep inside that the immoral relationship is out of your life. That anger may surface later and damage your attempts at restoration. It would be better to admit that the immoral relationship, though wrong, was a part of your life that you now grieve over. You may experience a "sense" of real pain for some time with regard to that relationship. Knowing that this feeling is part of grief, acknowledge it and move on. This approach is much healthier than denying that you feel loss at all.

It would be better to talk about this, if you need to, with a trusted friend instead of your spouse. A spouse can experience great additional pain if faced with your pain of the loss of an immoral relationship. To openly and honestly admit that you are working through obvious changes in your thinking and behavior is one thing. But to tell your spouse that you are missing a lost love is inflicting additional pain on your already hurt partner.

It is also helpful to understand that the loss of the immoral relationship will, in the end, result in better health for you. My mother, obviously very eager to keep her leg, understood that the gangrene that had infected her foot made it necessary to remove the leg. She knew that to avoid the painful process of amputating the leg would result in eventual decay of her whole body.

Immorality, less evident than gangrene on the skin, is unhealthy. If allowed to remain in a life, it causes decay of the soul. But the loss of the relationship, though painful, will result in restored health.

If you are the offended

If you are married to someone who has been unfaithful, then you are called to rise to a high level of Christian maturity. The term "self-sacrifice" will take on a new meaning. God allows for divorce in some cases of unfaithfulness, but He also says that He hates divorce. While there is biblical allowance for divorce, you are to be commended if you are willing to work out the difficulties and stay in the marriage.

The way you view yourself will be significant in relation to the way you view your spouse. In the next chapter, we will look at the role of the person who has been offended. Here we are concentrating on the way you view yourself.

One wife whose husband had been unfaithful told me that she felt dirty when she found out that he had been with another woman. Even though he was the one who defiled the marriage, she felt as if she had also had contact with the adulterous woman.

In another case, a man told me that his self-image was shattered when he found that his wife was unfaithful. His self-worth was based on having the model wife. Even though the event remained private, he felt as if everyone was looking at him and seeing a failure.

Feelings of rejection are almost always part of the emotional reaction of the offended party. This may result in feelings of inadequacy and guilt for the actions of the straying partner.

It is important to realize that you are not responsible for another person's actions. Of course, you may have indirectly contributed to your spouse's reasons leading up to the actions, but he is free to choose his own course, and is thus responsible for his actions.

There is always terrible pain for the recipient of unfaithfulness. That pain is normal. It is not a reflection of you as a person. You are a worthwhile human being before the Lord—fully accepted by Him through your relationship with His Son. Because He accepts you, you can accept yourself. Acceptance of self will enable you to accept your spouse.

Be careful not to wallow in a pity party. It would not be difficult, since you have been wronged, to assume the role of a martyr. If you think of yourself as a martyr, you will become almost unapproachable. The progress of restoration will be greatly impaired if you seem self-righteous and unforgiving.

Try to see yourself as a person totally loved and accepted by God. You are freely choosing, because of His love and acceptance, to stay in a painful relationship and work on restoration. You are not doing this because your spouse is worthy of such treatment. You are also not doing it because you are so superspiritual that you can conquer anything. You are doing it out of love and obedience to the Lord.

You need also to see yourself as a person who needs to grieve those difficult personal losses. Even though you still have your marriage, the relationship has certainly suffered loss. Loss of trust, innocence, romantic joy.

Admitting this and allowing yourself feelings that range from anger to acceptance will help heal your damaged emotions.

If you are single

If you are single and are at the end of an immoral relationship, you have the added pain of being alone. If no one else knows of your relationship, you may tend to hide the pain and go on as normal. But be willing to let a friend come alongside you and walk with you through this difficult time. Not only will a friend's presence be a comfort, but it will provide the kind of accountability you will need.

Just as in the case of the married person, you will need to live with the pain of the awareness of your sin. You will need to lay the guilt aside and move on. And, you will need to determine your lifestyle. If you don't want to find yourself in the same situation again, you will have to make changes in your thinking, behavior, and involvement. It will be a little harder for you than for the married person because you are working this out alone.

Feast on thoughts of your security and significance in the Lord. Focus on your relationship with Christ and His love for you.

It is an uphill battle—*but* it can be conquered. It is certainly worth the effort.

Christian husband after reconciliation with his wife: "One of the best things to do is to go for counseling. It helps you recognize the differences in the two of you that you may not be aware of.

"One of the biggest problems I had was the lack of trust my wife had in me. In the beginning of restoration, it was a problem if I said anything about what had happened, and it was a problem if I didn't. It got back to our lack of communication. So, I worked on communicating more and doing anything I could to help my wife regain confidence in me and in herself."

Another Christian husband after reconciliation with his wife: "I give full credit to my wife. After a brief separation, she received me back in warmly and even passionately. It was amazing to me. I felt unworthy of her, so she took the aggressive role."

Christian wife after reconciliation with her husband: "It was really hard for me in the beginning to trust my husband again. I always wondered when I went to the store, or even when I was taking a bath, if he was calling the woman he had been involved with. That was something I really had to trust God with. I had to pray a lot. The toughest thing for me is that my trust in my husband has been destroyed."

TWENTY-FIVE
Rebuilding Your Life

It was about ten in the evening when the phone rang. I answered it, wondering who would be calling at that hour.

"Rick isn't home yet," the familiar voice sobbed.

My friend, whose husband had recently ended an affair, was in a state of panic. Her voice was full of fear. She had waited two hours past his expected arrival home before calling me.

"He said he would be working till around eight. I can't call him because the office line is on an answering machine after five. I can't go over without waking the kids and dragging them along. I am trying to stay calm," her voice faded, turning into stifled sobs. I could feel her pain over the phone lines. She had suffered greatly, forgiven him, had determined to rebuild her marriage, and was trying to adjust to living in pain.

"I am *trying* to be rational. I really want to believe him. But—*where* is he?"

We talked for a while. She calmed down some. Rick finally came home while we were still on the phone.

The next morning my friend called to apologize for her hysterical call the night before. She went on to explain that Rick had been at work and had not called because the whole phone system at the office was out of order. Not only could she not call in; he could not call out.

As I listened to her, I felt suspicion enter my own thinking. Was he telling the truth? Suppose he *was* telling the truth. Did I have a right to doubt him? What should I say to my friend who now felt an element of relief, but who was in total agony the night before?

She went on to say that her relief was mixed with fear. She wanted to believe and had acted to him as if she had believed. But deep inside—she wondered.

After the affair

What happens within a home after the discovery of infidelity? What happens when a man and woman decide to stay together and work on rebuilding their marriage?

The intensity and complexity of emotions in such a home are enormous. Each family touched by this situation has its own set of unique circumstances. The personalities alone cause differences. There is no way to state "what happens" accurately because of this complexity.

Being careful, therefore, not to put any couple in a well-defined box, let's look at the similarities. Then perhaps we can better understand how to handle them, which may help in the restoration process.

Trust has been destroyed. Why? Because infidelity requires lies. Even if the lies are lies of omission, they are still lies. Infidelity means the breaking of a promise. We promise when we marry to be faithful, and we trust in our partner's promise to do the same.

When that promise is broken—even if we somehow suspected that it might happen—then trust is destroyed. Resentment and anger become constant companions of the offended party.

The person who was unfaithful experiences guilt and anger as well. His or her anger may be toward God, the spouse, or the partner in the adultery.

So, now you have a home where two people live (with their children, if they have any) in the midst of distrust, anger, guilt, and resentment.

And—life goes on. With emotional tensions at a peak, we feel as if we must take ourselves out of life for a while and have nothing else to deal with but those emotions. But we still have jobs and children and the affairs of everyday life. It may be necessary to dramatically slow down in those areas, but energy is required to find a way to do even that. To say that the whole situation is difficult is a gross understatement.

Infidelity is so common today that we may think of it as more "normal" than it really is. It is not what is supposed to be. The fact that a large number of people experience it does not lessen its devastation.

We need to accept the enormity of our problem. And, with aggressive determination, we need to accept the enormity of our God. Without Him, the prospects of restoration are dim. With Him, they are unlimited. God does not sweep down and heal instantly. He does not take all the pain away. But He does do supernatural things in the hearts of those who belong to Him.

He takes broken hearts and hard hearts and restores them. He takes broken lives and makes them whole in fantastic, unforeseeable ways. He takes our shattered dreams and replaces them with new contentment.

The ingredients He needs to accomplish these miracles in our lives are repentance, forgiveness, commitment, a decision to put Him first, lives yielded to Him in the middle of excruciating pain, and time.

The process toward restoration may be very long and very painful.

The process toward restoration

In Chapters 14 and 15, we have looked at the way back toward godliness. Restoration begins there. We need to be in a right relationship with God in order to be in right relationships with others.

In review, we need to:

- make a decision to put the relationship with Jesus Christ first in our lives;
- acknowledge our sin;
- take action to end an immoral relationship;
- take action based on obedience, not feelings;
- get out of the involvement—cold turkey;
- enter a relationship of accountability;
- recognize if addiction is present and seek help; and
- recognize Satan and his role in our sin.

With all these factors operating in our lives, the remaining element is *time*. The toughest part of the healing process is that it takes so long. Sometimes a lifetime.

Taking time—waiting on God and being patient—requires us to grow to new heights of maturity. We cannot be spoiled children demanding instant gratification. It can seem so comfortable to just remain a baby Christian. Sitting in the secure nest of our salvation, at first we might want to hold on to our spiritual infancy until our bodies are old and we just slip into heaven.

But those days are over. We are no longer babies, and we are not working through a baby problem. We are out of the nest and into the big league process of sanctification.

We need to be healed and be restored and grow, because that is a major part of God's plan for us. He does not want us to remain as children. Growing in maturity is a way of saying that we are becoming more like Jesus. Jesus wants our marriages to be restored. But first we must decide to mature to the level that we *will* endure that process.

Howard Hendricks once gave an illustration on the "high-water mark of maturity." He told about a young woman some years ago whose husband was reported missing in Viet Nam. At first she said that she had to learn to live with the fact that her husband might be dead. After some time passed and he was still missing, she said that she had to learn to live with the fact that he might still be alive. But after years passed, she had to learn to live with the fact that she would never know. "That," said Dr. Hendricks, "is the high-water mark of maturity."

We may never again know the peace of living in a relationship untouched by the pain of unfaithfulness. It takes a high-water mark of maturity to be willing to stay in the process of restoration, not knowing the end result. The woman whose husband was still missing in Viet Nam had no choice. Her circumstances were dictated to her. She did have a choice in her response to them. She chose to accept them and live well through them.

But most of us have a choice. When we choose to head toward restoration, we demonstrate maturity by our willingness to walk a long, hard road for an infinite amount of time.

There is no step-by-step procedure toward restoration. There are a lot of ups and downs happening at the same time. There will be good days; there will be bad ones. Emotions will be in control, and then run out of control.

In the middle of this mess, what we need to constantly

remember is to put our relationship with Christ first. Our difficult situation can so consume us that we forget our anchor in Him. No matter what else happens, our relationship with Christ remains secure. As we choose to walk obediently with Him, He will unravel the mess of our lives.

There are some practical things we can do to aid in restoration. Let's look at them, remembering that to focus on them and forget the Lord will result in an empty effort. These suggestions will be helpful if He is the center of our thinking and actions.

Communication

"Then we will no longer be infants, tossed back and forth by the waves, and blown here and there by every wind of teaching and by the cunning and craftiness of men in their deceitful scheming. Instead, *speaking the truth in love,* we will in all things grow up into him who is the Head, that is, Christ" (Ephesians 4:14-15).

A relationship fractured by immorality has suffered a lack of truth and a lack of love. But the Word of God challenges us to commit our lives to the process of communication by "speaking the truth in love." Speaking the truth means no more lies. Speaking in love means a lack of anger and malice, and a concern for the other person. It does not mean that we communicate *every* thought.

We may still *feel* that we love the person with whom we were involved. But to communicate that to a wounded spouse is not loving. The truth is, although we may still have feelings for the other person, we have chosen to be committed to our marriage. A true commitment to marriage is a reality upon which we will act in love. "I still have feelings for the other person" is an emotion that may still exist in our thinking, but upon which we will not act.

In this process of communicating, we need to make a verbal commitment to our spouse to be faithful in the task of restoring the marriage. If we are the wounded party, we need to communicate to our spouse our forgiveness and commitment to the marriage.

We need to openly communicate about the need for counseling. Adultery is usually a symptom of a much deeper problem. To end one relationship and fail to see the root cause of it will not really heal the situation. Christian counseling can uncover that root problem and aid toward more complete healing.

Roller-coaster emotions

A friend shared with me that one of the most difficult things for her to handle in the restoration process in her marriage was her up-and-down emotions.

"I felt such passion for my husband," she expressed, "after he ended his affair and we began to work on our relationship. It was like being on our honeymoon again. We were like two kids in love. Then, out of the blue, the doubts would come back and haunt me. I felt mad at him. I didn't want him near me. Time would pass—and the passion would return. It's a roller coaster."

Emotions are unstable factors. That doesn't mean that they are bad or good. Simply unstable.

It is normal to feel a rush of excitement when you start to rebuild. There has been a battle, and you have won. But then the scars from the battle begin to hurt, and the initial rush is gone.

Just to know that emotions will run wild will help. Decide ahead of time not to jump to hasty action based on emotion. Decide not to end the effort toward restoration merely because you *feel* discouraged or doubtful. While restored passion is good, you shouldn't conclude that all your problems are over and you're completely out of the woods.

Emotions will rise and fall. Stay committed to the Lord and what He is doing in your marriage.

Suggestions for the offender

1. *Remind yourself that your actions are based on commitment, not on the response of your spouse.*

2. *When feelings of guilt begin to incapacitate you, persevere in your determination to make it work this time.*

> We may, indeed, be sure that perfect chastity—like perfect charity—will not be attained by any merely human efforts. You must ask for God's help. Even when you have done so, it may seem to you for a long time that no help, or less help than you need, is being given. Never mind. After each failure, ask forgiveness, pick yourself up, and try again. Very often what God first helps us towards is not the virtue itself but just this power of always trying again.[17]

3. *Be vulnerable.*

> For us fidelity has much broader connotations than absolute sexual loyalty. In the best relationships there will be a fidelity of sharing. We pledge ourselves to travel the inner roads together. We will take off our masks, come out from behind our facades. We will be honest with each other.[18]

4. *Be sensitive to your spouse's fears.* If you are going to be late getting home, call. Don't set up situations to test your spouse's trust. Trust has to be rebuilt.

5. *Put romance back into the marriage relationship again.*

6. *Don't respond to questions from your spouse about details of the adulterous relationship.* There may be a tendency on the part of your spouse to want to know *exactly* what happened between you and the other party. It is difficult to forget what is described in detail, and it serves no healthy or restoring purpose.

7. *Begin to rebuild a spiritual focus in the home.*

Suggestions for the offended

1. *Remember that your commitment to the marriage is based on your relationship with Jesus Christ and is not dependent on your spouse's response.*

2. *Do not be sarcastic.* Hurt and anger may surface in the form of sarcasm. But sarcasm only tears down and slows the healing process.

3. *Don't interrogate your spouse.* You may have a curiosity about exactly what went on between your spouse and the other person, but resist the temptation to question.

4. *Be vulnerable.* Express your feelings in love without making demands. Because you are the one who has been offended, you may feel that you have the right to make demands. But be open and not demanding.

5. *Reach out to your spouse in small ways if you are unable to reach out in large ones.* Basically, show a loving attitude.

6. *Don't bring up the sins of the past.*

7. *Show a forgiving spirit.* Scripture tells us, "Bear with each other and forgive whatever grievances you may have against one another. Forgive as the Lord forgave you" (Colossians 3:13). The word "for-

give" here means to freely pardon with a sense of kindness. Now, you may feel that your spouse doesn't deserve to be pardoned. That may be true. But we are told to forgive as the Lord forgave us. And that forgiveness was based on His love, not on our worthiness. Even if we don't feel forgiving, we can display a forgiving spirit.

Future hope

The future may look a little grim right now. That does not mean that it *is* grim. We are called to walk by faith, not by sight. It is not important what you can see, but rather what you do.

If you have chosen to make your relationship with Christ first in your life, then you are on the right track. Your faith will grow as you honor Him by a true commitment to your marriage.

PART IX

Moving On

TWENTY-SIX

What Should Our Response Be?

We are attacked on every side. In the newspapers, on television, in sarcastic lyrics of songs, and verbally by those eager to throw stones at the Christian community.

How are we to respond in our own thinking to attacks upon Christians who have been exposed for their sexual immorality?

The first natural response when we hear of a case of immorality, whether it is someone we know personally or a Christian celebrity, is that of shock. We are surprised. We are caught off guard. We may have been living with the assumption that committed Christians do not get involved in that kind of sin. And now we are faced with an account, and an admission, that a committed Christian has become ensnared. It *is* shocking. May we never become so used to sin that we are not surprised when an image-bearer of the Lord Jesus Christ falls.

Our shock should not lead us to bitterness and judgment. It should lead to grief. Whatever the circumstances of the particular person may be, there is cause for deeply felt grief that a fellow brother or sister in the Lord has darkened the name of Christ and his or her own name.

As we sit in front of our televisions and watch the very foundation of our lives being torn down publicly, our hearts ache at all the misunderstanding that inevitably results. Some people who do not know the Lord will, of course, judge Him based on His followers. They will not have any knowledge of the doctrine of grace and forgiveness. They will draw conclusions about a relationship with the

Lord based on incomplete information. It is important, therefore, for those of us who *do* know the meaning of grace and forgiveness to be more outspoken than ever before.

We should speak in meek and gentle ways to the attackers of Christianity, but we do need to take a stand. To the unbelieving world, we need to lift up the Lord in spite of the way His people let Him down. There is no room to join the stone throwers. Whether someone is right or wrong is not the issue when talking with an unbeliever. The issue is the continued validity of an authentic relationship with the God of the universe.

When in the company of other believers, there is a great temptation to join in on the latest gossip. It is hard not to. We are all affected by the media coverage Christianity now receives. There is no doubt that we need ways to dialogue together in working through our own reactions to what is happening around us.

But we need to be careful. We need to make sure we are not causing younger believers to stumble by our remarks. And any one of us might be the next person exposed. None of us are exempt from temptation. Even in private conversations, we need to bring our thoughts back to Christ and His mercy and forgiveness.

How, then, do we reconcile 1 Corinthians 5:11 with 2 Corinthians 2:5-8?

> You must not associate with anyone who calls himself a brother but is sexually immoral or greedy, an idolater or a slanderer, a drunkard or a swindler. With such a man do not even eat. (1 Corinthians 5:11)

> If anyone has caused grief, he has not so much grieved me as he has grieved all of you, to some extent—not to put it too severely. The punishment inflicted on him by the majority is sufficient for him. Now instead, you ought to forgive and comfort him, so that he will not be overwhelmed by excessive sorrow. I urge you, therefore, to reaffirm your love for him. (2 Corinthians 2:5-8)

The attitude of the person who has behaved immorally determines our response. In a word—*repentance.* If a person continues to sin and remains in fellowship with believers, the believers are called upon to confront him or her. We, as brothers and sisters in Christ, are offended by the sins of others in the family. The familiar procedure is found in the words of Jesus:

> "If your brother sins against you, go and show him his fault, just between the two of you. If he listens to you, you have won your brother over. But if he will not listen, take one or two others along, so that 'every matter may be established by the testimony of two or three witnesses.' If he refuses to listen to them, tell it to the church; and if he refuses to listen even to the church, treat him as you would a pagan or a tax collector." (Matthew 18:15-17)

Harsh words.

This issue is complicated for us personally because this procedure is often short-circuited in midstream. Often we confront someone and he doesn't change. Not wanting to be intruders, we let the matter drop. Because we so often don't follow through with discipline from the church, we are at a loss to be effective on an individual level.

As individual church members, we don't ban people from our congregations. We then have to determine what we will do as far as continuing with the offending brother or sister. I don't have a pat answer here. Each case is different. There are as many variables as there are cases of immorality.

We have to go before the Lord and prayerfully consider what He would have us do in relating to this particular person. Sometimes what we do depends on our role or position with this person.

But what about the verses in 2 Corinthians regarding forgiveness and comfort? That passage also mentions that "the punishment inflicted on him by the majority is sufficient for him." Obviously, this offender has submitted to church discipline. That would indicate an apparent attitude of repentance. Even if a person is not called before the church for discipline, he may be truly repentant.

Repentance calls for forgiveness and restoration. We need to lovingly reach out to this wounded brother or sister. Reaching out does not mean that we approve of this person's sin. It means that we accept him or her as a person. It is the same kind of love as the love bestowed on us by the Lord.

Response when the person is not close to us

Our response will naturally vary according to our relationship with the person who has been exposed in immorality. Suppose the person is someone we do not know personally at all. He or she is a Christian "name" that has been exposed by the press and media.

We should feel our deepest grief whenever the name of the *Lord* is defaced. There is grief, too, at the damage that may have been done to a related ministry and to the people who have been faithful followers of that particular ministry.

In order to deal with our anger, we need to admit it to the Lord—and lay it aside. If we have no relation to the person involved, it is not our personal responsibility to determine discipline. We can pray for those to whom he or she is accountable, and then resume responsibility for ourselves.

Looking closely at our own lives may be the most effective thing we can do as Christians in a world where Christians are visibly falling. We all know the phrase, "There, but by the grace of God, go you or I." It is a humbling exercise to look intently at our own lives—in every area—and see how we can better walk with Christ.

Guarding one's own heart leaves little time to be overly concerned with the faults of others. In taking a stand for Christ, we need to lift Him up, not tear others down. We need to be personal examples of godliness, and leave judgment to the Lord.

Response when the person is close to us

When someone we know personally is exposed in immorality, we need to evaluate our role in that person's life.

In Christian businesses and in churches, there are (or should be) established procedures to deal with disobedience to the Lord. People in leadership are well aware of these procedures and their obligations to carry them out.

What if you are a coworker, not a logical agent of the biblical procedure of discipline? Again, it depends on your relationship with the person being disciplined. If you are already friends with that person, you need to be supportive of him in his attempt to live out the discipline. If you are not very close to this person, you should be warm and supportive, but not a curiosity seeker. Your prayers and the working of the Holy Spirit in your own life may be the most appropriate conduct for you to carry out.

Outside of church and the work place, you may have a close friend who is experiencing this kind of trauma. This is a great opportunity to reach out in Christian love. In Proverbs 15:4, we read, "The tongue that brings healing is a tree of life." This friend's wounds will need healing. If he is truly repentant, he will experience great pain in his process of restoration.

Being a comfort may mean listening. It may mean spending time with the person. If you are especially close, you may have the opportunity and responsibility of being the person to whom the wounded believer is accountable. This calls for close accounts in your own life. To walk next to a brother or sister in pain is a great privilege. It is also a great responsibility. This friend may be in such pain that he or she has difficulty seeing the Lord. To see Him in a person he or she trusts may be the first crucial step back to a right relationship before God.

Speaking the truth in love

I had lunch recently with a friend of mine who works for a Christian organization. She had observed some strange behavior by one of her coworkers with one of the men in leadership. We talked about it, and there seemed to be strong evidence that some inappropriate behavior was going on.

Stop.

Caution!

This sounds a lot like gossip.

Is it gossip?

What if there is not any inappropriate behavior?

What if there is?

This is dangerous ground. What is our responsibility and what is our limit in intruding in another's life?

James 5:19-20 says, "If one of you should wander from the truth and someone should bring him back, remember this: Whoever turns a sinner from the error of his way will save him from death and cover over a multitude of sins."

We need to be very careful that we speak the *truth* and that we speak it in *love.* The truth may be that it *appears* that something wrong is happening. Now, that is not saying that something wrong *is* happening, but that it *appears* that way. Speaking in love means that there is no delight in confronting someone about sin. There is concern. Concern for the person and for the name of Christ.

Confronting is not a popular pastime. We may meet with denial, rejection, or flat-out anger. The response of the person is not our responsibility. Our responsibility is to speak the truth in love. Being the brunt of someone's anger may be worth it if we save that person from falling. Although that person may not agree with us at the moment, he may be forced to think about where he really is in his walk with the Lord.

I have a friend who lost his position with a Christian organization because of adultery. He shared with me that while he was in the early stages of the adulterous relationship, he had an ability to compartmentalize his life. He had his spiritual life, and he had this secret side of his life. No one confronted him about his behavior. His behavior was not overtly immoral. But, had someone noticed the attention he was paying to the woman he became involved with, that person might have interrupted his ability to put his life in compartments. The pressure of knowing that others are aware of your actions can be a deterrent to continuing.

We are on the same side

There are no villains in black and good guys in white in this battle. As Christians, we are on the same side. We need to help each other.

We need to confront, forgive, reach out, and restore. And, we need to constantly lift up Jesus, to call out to Him, to talk about Him, to walk as He walked, and to love as He loves.

TWENTY-SEVEN

How to Have Proper Male-Female Relationships

I have several very close and healthy relationships with married men. I have a few close relationships with single men that are strictly platonic ones. For example, I have a close relationship with my divorced brother-in-law. These friendships are all meaningful and fulfilling. They are all free from any immoral implications at all.

One of my married friends is a writer. He has been a source of great encouragement to me—a mentor. We generally get together in a public restaurant and talk and talk. We talk of life and God and issues and what makes writers writers. I talk to his wife often on the phone, but rarely see her.

One of my single male friends and I used to work together. He had been a friend to both my husband and me before my husband was killed. Our friendship continued after I was widowed and, in fact, grew stronger. We never had a dating relationship, in fact neither of us has ever even mentioned it. Although we live a great distance apart, we are still in touch. When we are together, it is as if we just saw each other the day before—comfortable and trusting.

I don't have a brother, but I imagine if I did, I would feel about him the way I do about my brother-in-law. We no longer live in the same city, but we talk frequently and visit about once a year. My daughters and I stay with him when we go East, and he stays with us when he comes West.

There are a number of other men I know with whom I have a good, though not particularly close, relationship. There are others I relate to in some capacity, but would never even entertain the thought of a close friendship with them. What are the ingredients that need to exist in order to have healthy male-female friendships?

It begins with yourself.
When my relationship with the Lord is off track, all my other relationships suffer—not just the ones with men, but with my children, girlfriends, and acquaintances. "Off track" is usually a result of overlooking the basics and intently looking at my circumstances. The place to begin in having healthy male-female friendships is, again, in our relationship with Jesus Christ. If our fellowship with Him is broken, our minds and hearts are fertile soil for Satan's temptations.

That is not to say that temptation is gone when the relationship with the Lord is firm. Temptation is always right there with us *or* just around the corner.

Weaknesses I have experienced tend to remain weaknesses. What I do with them differs, but the weaknesses remain. There are certain qualities about men that make me turn my head, at least mentally. Even though I practice the guidelines mentioned earlier, the old nature still bubbles up at a whiff of a certain aftershave or a glance at a particular countenance. So—I talk to myself. I tell myself what specifically tempts me.

There are a number of unseen, or nonphysical, qualities that can be deceptively tempting. I say deceptive because the qualities may be very positive—godliness, wisdom, compassion, leadership ability—qualities that draw us to others. These qualities may be good, but we need to know how we personally respond to them. Ask yourself, "When I am in a group of people, what kind of person of the opposite sex do I enjoy talking to?" Recognize some of the qualities of that type of person—friendly, quiet, assertive, attentive.

Be aware of which "triggers" cause you to fantasize or linger mentally over someone. You need not avoid friendships with people who have a particular appeal, but be aware of areas where you have to check yourself quickly to prevent your mind from wandering.

Above all, don't tell your friends of the opposite sex about those things in them that tempt you. Admitting that we feel a certain chemistry with someone puts a terrible strain on maintaining a godly, healthy friendship.

When you find yourself with someone who causes your mind to have inappropriate thoughts, you need to discipline yourself very early in the relationship to kill those thoughts. If they grow, you jeopardize your ability to ever have a good friendship with that person. You simply cannot allow yourself to fantasize about someone, spend a lot of time with that person, and then expect everything to remain godly. Soon you will find yourself immersed in the process that leads to emotional dependency, and on to involvement.

In order to have good male-female friendships, we must not even play around with the beginning steps that may lead to immorality.

Look at the other person

If our relationship with the Lord is strong and another person of the opposite sex has a strong relationship with the Lord, we have a better chance to have a good friendship with that person. Remember, that is no guarantee, but at least we are on the same track.

It is also possible to have godly male-female friendships with unbelievers. The responsibility for the course of that friendship, however, rests with us. That may not seem fair, but a nonbeliever does not have the same commitment to morality that a believer should. There are many moral nonbelievers. They do not have the same power resource and motivation, however, when temptation enters the picture.

We need to have a firm conviction of the kind of friendship that will exist in this relationship and tactfully communicate that to the other person. My nonbelieving friends know where I stand. My nonbelieving male friends are all very respectful of that stand.

Once we determine that we will not "play with fire" with regard to any of the stages that lead to immorality, the elements of friendships are similar to those we maintain with members of the same sex: trust, respect, common interests.

Limited friendships

In this age of openness, we need to realize that all relationships operate within certain limits. We relate to relatives, coworkers, neighbors, and friends in a particular context. I speak to my children much more openly than I do to someone else's children. My relatives might see the inside of my house in a different state than my neighbors would—unless they dropped in unexpectedly.

In male-female friendships, there are limits. Sometimes, the closer we are, the greater are certain limits. I share a very close relationship with one of my married male friends. We *never* hug, exchange lingering looks, or say provocative things to each other. This restriction allows for a wonderful freedom.

How do we have freedom with such restriction? We have it because we trust each other, his wife trusts us, and God allows us to function freely within certain clearcut limits. We relate primarily on a work-related plane. We talk openly and deeply in that area, but we have no emotional dependency on each other. We do not dabble, even a little bit, in any area that may lead to anything improper.

Limits are good. They allow for godly interaction. Almost everything we live with is limited. Fire is good for cooking. It is not good if the flames leap above the stove and catch the ceiling on fire.

Sexual desires are good. They are good and fulfilling in the context of marriage. To bring those flames into a friendship, where they should not be expressed, is damaging. It burns down the relationship with the Lord, the other person, your spouse, your children, and on and on.

If you happen to be single and thus do not have the arena of marriage to express your sexual desires, you have to be especially careful what you convey to friends of the opposite sex. You may need to fight more intensely to keep your focus on the Lord. You *will* need to fight more intensely the desire to "play."

When you are not in a marriage relationship (or if you are in an unhealthy marriage), you will be strongly tempted to see if you can still generate interest from the opposite sex. That desire exists even for people who are in good marriages. But it is stronger for the person who is not getting any human confirmation of his or her desirability. You simply cannot bring that kind of fishing or teasing into a friendship and expect it to grow in a godly way.

Enjoy the Lord with others

How wonderful it is to enjoy the Lord with another believer. We can have meaningful and lasting friendships when our chief desire in that friendship is to be God's man and God's woman.

We have an opportunity to be encouragers from the Lord in the lives of others. As soon as we cross over from that motivation to one of selfish desires, we become instruments of Satan in the life of our friend.

If we are romantically involved with someone, we certainly don't feel like we could possibly be instruments of Satan. But we are. Anytime we contribute to someone's sinning, we are not on the Lord's side in that person's life. We have opened the door for Satan to get a foothold—not only on that person, but on us.

Godly friendships between men and women are a blessing to be enjoyed. We lose the opportunity for that blessing when we allow those friendships to be destroyed by immorality.

To keep friendships godly:

- look at yourself and your relationship with the Lord;
- look at the other person and his or her character;
- establish limits and stick to them;
- don't tell the other person of temptations you have with him or her;
- focus on the Lord; and
- be an encourager for the Lord in the life of the other person, not an instrument of Satan.

PART X

To Begin

TWENTY-EIGHT

The Passionate Life

"Going a little farther, [Jesus] fell with his face to the ground and prayed, 'My Father, if it is possible, may this cup be taken from me. Yet not as I will, but as you will'" (Matthew 26:39).

Jesus, God the Son, in the Garden of Gethsemane—fell to the ground on His face!

Have you ever been flat on the ground before God? Broken?

If you have not, then the truly passionate life has not been part of your experience, either. Oh, we can experience worldly passion for worldly things. But the passion one experiences when broken before God is not of this world.

When Jesus was on His face in the garden, He gave us our highest example of a life filled with passion. He suffered what we cannot describe with words—willingly—at the hands of His Father—for us.

Are we not moved to the point of revulsion when we think of the connotation of the word "passion" today? One of the meanings of passion *is* related to sexual desire. But in our society that has become the *only* meaning. To be a passionate person implies that we are sexually expressive in an intense way. To be less than that, according to the world, is to be something less than whole.

To live with a measure of full joy means to have a passion for Christ. We have talked much in this book about a relationship with Christ. But, as the saying goes, "Mere talk leads only to poverty."

There is no poverty worse than poverty of the soul. Our entire world suffers from poverty of the soul, and that world doesn't even know it. Until we see Jesus on His face before His Father, *we* do not see our *own* poverty! To have someone who is sovereign give Himself to that measure for us—and for us to be less than passionate about that sacrifice—is poverty of the soul.

We have to peer into the garden, and then look up from the foot of the Cross, in order to understand the Resurrection. We have to get down on our face before God and surrender to His will. We have to embrace the Cross to feel His blood spilled for us personally. Only then can we have the fullness of joy over life eternal.

Mere talk is useless. Our thoughts, behavior, and involvements have to line up with a passion for Christ—*if* we want to have a truly passionate life.

All the passion of the worldly scene is dust compared to one moment in the presence of the Lord, when we *know* we are fully loved and accepted. This moment may be experienced differently by different people. It may come in a very emotional way, or calmly. It may be repeated frequently, or just be a moment here, a moment there.

Living in a passionate relationship with God is not definable in words. There is no prescription one can take to achieve the desired result. It is not a once in a lifetime decision to do this or that, to live this list and throw out that one.

It is a journey. It may have begun for you years ago. It may not yet have started. If we are sidetracked in our journey, gazing at the desires of this world, then our passion for Christ will suffer. And our joy in Him will be diminished.

What is important is to begin.

Notes

1. "A Talk with the MacDonalds," *Christianity Today* (July 10, 1987), page 38.
2. Jeffrey Meyers, *Hemingway: A Biography* (New York: Harper & Row, Publishers, Inc., 1985), page 145.
3. Andrew Murray, *The Believer's Secret of Waiting on God* (Minneapolis: Bethany House Publishers, 1986), page 16.
4. Frank B. Minirth, M.D., and Paul D. Meier, M.D., *Happiness Is a Choice* (Grand Rapids: Baker Book House, 1978), page 51.
5. William MacDonald, *True Discipleship* (Kansas City, Kans.: Walterick Publishers, 1975), pages 33-34; used by permission of Walterick Publishers.
6. Taken from *My Heart—Christ's Home* by Robert Boyd Munger, revised edition, copyright 1986 by Inter-Varsity Christian Fellowship of the U.S.A. and used by permission of InverVarsity Press, P.O. Box 1400, Downers Grove, Illinois 60515.
7. W. Somerset Maugham, *The Razor's Edge* (New York: Penguin Books in the United States of America by arrangement with Doubleday & Company, Inc., 1943, 1944), page 54.
8. Lawrence J. Crabb, Jr., *The Marriage Builder* (Grand Rapids: Zondervan Publishing House, 1982), page 29.
9. Charles Colson, *Dare to Be Different, Dare to Be a Christian* (Wheaton, Ill.: Victor Books, a division of Scripture Press Publications, Inc., 1986), page 1.
10. George Howe Colt (text), Marsha Dubrow, Edward Barnes, Vic-

toria Balfour (reporting), "*Life* Polls America: Sex and the Presidency," *Life*, Volume 10, Number 8 (August 1987), pages 70-75.

11. Ninon d'Enclos (c. 1700).
12. Jerry B. Jenkins, "Of Scandals and Hedges," *Moody Monthly*, Volume 87, Number 11 (July/August 1987), page 6; used by permission of Jerry Jenkins.
13. Elisabeth Elliot, *A Chance to Die* (Old Tappan, N.J.: Fleming H. Revell Company, 1987), page 59.
14. Elliot, *A Chance to Die*, page 79.
15. Charles Haddon Spurgeon, *The Treasury of David*, Volume 2 (McLean, Va.: MacDonald Publishing Company), pages 88-94.
16. "A Talk with the MacDonalds," *Christianity Today*, page 38.
17. C.S. Lewis, *The Four Loves* (New York: Harcourt Brace Jovanovich, Inc., 1960).
18. Charlie and Martha Shedd, *Celebration in the Bedroom* (Waco, Tex.: Word Publishers, 1979).